Germania's Assault Generation

Germania's Assault Generation

Germania's Assault Generation

"History is always written by the victor, and the histories of the losing parties belong to the shrinking circle of those who were there..."

SS-Standartenführer Jochen Peiper – 1. SS-Panzer-Division "Leibstandarte Adolf Hitler"

Contents

Foreword 7

A Word from the Author...9

Acknowledgements 13

Introduction 17

The Legionnaires...23

Rottenführer Martti Lehtonen – FFB/4.kp – Finnisches
Freiwilligen Bataillon der Waffen SS/4. Kp. 37

From the Frw. Standarte Nordwest to the Germanic SS
in Flanders 94

Schwerer Granatwerfer Zug – 4.Kp/I. Btl/67. Rgt/
III. SS-Panzer-Korps...105

A War Volunteer with the Hitlerjugend Division....................124

From Demjansk to Breslau – 3.SS-Panzer-Division -
"Totenkopf"..147

The Panzerjäger of Das Reich 165

Götterdämmerung – the Last Moments of the
33.Waffen-Grenadier-Division der SS - "Charlemagne" 194

Endnote - The Waffen SS 207

Das Kreuz im Hürtgenwald 215

In Memoriam:...216

The 38 Divisions of the Waffen SS...217

Germania's Assault Generation

References - Sources..221

Foreword

I am absolutely honored to introduce you to Gerry Villani and his latest work of art. Gerry's focus has always been on telling the stories that no one else will tell, giving a voice to those that no one has listened to, and doing it in a way that others have not. With his last book *"Soldiers of Germania, the European Volunteers of the Waffen SS"*, he gave us insight into the experiences of men from all across Europe who volunteered to serve as foreign SS soldiers. The story he brought to us is one that many do not know. It is commonly implied that the German Army, and German soldiers, were all of undiluted German heritage, when in fact men from over 30 countries served in the SS. Gerry has granted us access to the lives and perspectives which are unique and widely unknown to the world.

The route that many stories throughout history take is a path that from far away looks smooth and truly has been worn into a comfortable retelling of events. Once again Gerry stepped off the beaten path and into the weeds. He has compiled through personal research the up close and personal stories that many are too afraid to tell or be associated with. We find him in the trenches with the soldiers. We find him sitting in the shadows of conflict. He diligently transcribed the stories of these veterans, stories which have long gone untold - buried in the depths of memory, or whispered through the din of battle, nearly lost in the fog of war. I picture him, but a silhouette, following closely behind these soldiers as they say goodbye to their families and march towards their destiny. What Gerry has done for history is invaluable and what he has done for these men is unparalleled. But a glaring question still remains...why? Why would someone go through the troubles of searching the world for the tales of a few men whose lives have been eagerly forgotten by the people they once fought to protect? What makes a man voluntarily suffer the loss of sleep, time with loved ones, and his peace of mind - only to spend months chasing ghosts?

For Gerry the fascination with mankind's penchant for conflict started at a young age. Whenever he visited his grandparents, he was regaled with stories of the war. First-hand accounts of battle and the impact that war had on the world enchanted Gerry. Peering through the eyes of his grandparents, he learned that the actions of individual men created and shaped the world we live in today. Seeing that the individual - when helped by fate, luck, and chance - could affect not only his surroundings, but the globe, would start Gerry down a path in life from which he would never divert. With his latest book *"Germania's Assault Generation"*, we will be brought back into a world at war, where men of many nations believed in a united Europe, and joined the Waffen SS with enthusiasm in hopes of accomplishing that goal they believed in. We read the stories of Legionnaires, people of so-called "Germanic descent", who originated from occupied territories. With an insight into the motivations and internal conflicts that these volunteering soldiers went through, how their cultural backgrounds affected their positions in the military, and the way they viewed conflict and battle, this book is another unique take on the soldiers who fought in World War Two. I know that you will enjoy this book as much as I did, and it is my absolute privilege to present to you "Germania's Assault Generation".

Jennifer Georg, Ohio, August 2017

A Word from the Author

When the final battle was fought and the dead are gathered on the battlefields, a lonely soldier was found on the side of a hill. This soldier took up position behind a tree, with on the ground right next to him, several clips of ammunition for his rifle as a silent witness to his decision: to hold his position or to die. He died. The soldier lost his life on the side of the hill as a bullet had penetrated his head right under his steel helmet. When silence had taken over again on the hill and on the battlefield, the soldier was still sitting there in position with his rifle at the ready…ready to fire. He was still waiting patiently for the enemy to arrive, an enemy he'd ultimately never see. A lonely soldier was sitting on the side of the hill whose courage became him fatal. A soldier like any other soldier in the world. Most people like to call them SS monsters, although SS Mann would be more appropriate for Waffen SS soldiers. To call them all SS monsters is just an ignorant way to look at the history of the Waffen SS. Lots of Waffen SS soldiers only heard after the war that they were called fanatics, but that word was unknown to them during the war. Instead they were good soldiers, hard soldiers, and hard-fighting soldiers. The will of fighting was necessary to the last. Every man was willing to sacrifice himself, but whether this was fanatic or not I'll leave that up to you. Some people may call it that way but it still remains a strange word. It was certainly not a word that was used by the Waffen SS soldiers. They called it the love for the fatherland and for their people! These men were called the assault generation of Germania, or greater Germany, and they had largely been born in the years during and after World War I. Coming from every nation of Europe, they had risen up against communism and banded together under one flag for a common cause. They joined the German Army in World War II, a volunteer army that was better known as the Waffen SS. And it was in the Waffen SS, the elite fighting force of Germany, where the first modern European army was born. A new society of front fighters emerged from many different European nations; it was a society that had been forged in the sacrifice, sweat, and blood on the battlefield. Maybe their heritage and culture was different, but their uniforms and motto were one and the same: Meine Ehre Heißt Treue! SS soldiers were held to higher standards than regular Wehrmacht soldiers in the German Army, and the SS was subjected to the strictest discipline. For example, sentences handed down by SS courts were more severe than sentences passed by other courts for the same offense. A separate wing on the east side of the bunker (camp prison) at Dachau was reserved for SS soldiers who had committed a criminal act. This section has been torn down and can no longer be seen at the Dachau Memorial Site. When Dachau was liberated on April 29, 1945, there were still 128 SS men incarcerated in the Dachau bunker. They were released and given the job of guarding the prisoners until the American liberators arrived. Most of the regular guards at Dachau had fled the night before the camp was liberated. In 1943, a Waffen SS officer named Dr. Georg Konrad Morgen, who was also an attorney, was authorized by Himmler to conduct investigations into corruption and brutality in the concentration camps. Around 800 investigations of the SS were conducted, which resulted in around 200 indictments. At the Nuremberg International Military Tribunal, SS Lt. General Ernst Kaltenbrunner testified that there were 13 Stammlager (main concentration camps) in the Nazi camp system. One of these camps was Matzgau, located near Danzig; it was a camp where SS guards were imprisoned for offenses such as physical mistreatment of concentration camp prisoners, embezzlement, or theft. Yet tour guides at Dachau routinely tell visitors that the guards could do anything they wanted to with regard to abusing or killing the prisoners.

A Word from the Author

When looking at the Waffen SS volunteer, it can be said that there is no such thing as a pattern that can be extrapolated as being the main reason for enlistment in the Waffen SS. There's that image, often romanticized by the post war literature, of the Catholic crusader who wanted to fight Bolshevism. However there were many factors, often personal, that played a major role in the decision to join this new army: political division in one's country of origin, escapism, the sense of adventure, the need for a job, etc., but above all, the look and appeal of the Waffen SS was very attractive. The terms Waffen SS and Nazis have been used interchangeably, and the actual history is often confused. Certainly, being a veteran of the Waffen SS does not equate to being a Nazi. Many people that study the Waffen SS usually emphasize that most of their members were conscripted, i.e., its members had no choice. For how many of its members this is correct, we do not know.

This is my third book about the soldiers of the Waffen SS, and I realize that I'm riding that razor edge again. In fact, you ride it all the time when you write about the German armed forces of WWII, especially the Waffen SS. However, one has to be able to look at both sides of the stories, and that is what I'm doing. It's not a justification about the crimes that some of the units or brigades had committed nor is it to support the ideologies of a regime that was responsible for the killings of millions of people. The social-psychological side of Nazism and the persecution of Jews and other religious or ethnic groups is complex and thoroughly studied for many years, but it remains difficult in this modern day and age to draw a nuanced picture of the Waffen SS volunteer. The fascination with "the greatest crime of all times" - the holocaust - and the attraction that Nazism had at that time on the people still remains in the generations after the war. Mostly because phenomena such as discrimination, abuse of power, and violence are still the order of the day. You just

Germania's Assault Generation

have to turn on your TV or read a newspaper. With this new book, I hope that historians and students alike will be able to understand the motivation of the European volunteers of the Waffen SS, and that one can see beyond the stigma of monsters or murderers which has been bestowed upon them for the past 7 decades.

To conclude I can say that all wars end up being reduced to statistics, strategies, debates about their origins and results. These debates about war are important, but not more important than the human story of those who fought in them. Ordinary men conscripted into the Heer, Luftwaffe and Kriegsmarine or enlisted men of the Waffen SS did not fight for the NSDAP (Nationalsozialistische Deutsche Arbeiterpartei). Neither did the hundreds of thousands of European volunteers. There were certainly other values and beliefs involved. Perspectives that may be easily forgotten.

Gerry Villani, Okotoks, August 2017

Acknowledgements

This project couldn't have been completed without the help of some very important people. Their help, moral support, providing of crucial documents and documentation, and giving me permission to use some of their personal materials was crucial for the accomplishment of this work. You can't build an empire on your own! A very special thank you goes to:

Jennifer Brady, my sister from Facebook. A very smart lady who wrote a masterpiece of a foreword for this book. I'm truly honored Jen!

Jaana Lehtonen, granddaughter of Martti Lehtonen, for providing me with the story of her hero and giving me permission to use it. Also a big thank you to Ville Hacklin for translating the diary/story.

Tomasz Borowski, my Polish brother and author of "*Last Blood on Pomerania: Leon Degrelle and the Walloon Waffen SS Volunteers, February-May 1945*", for his support and providing me with essential information for the completion of my book!

My brother Chadwick Clark for being my editor. Thank you so much for taking the time to review my work and making it look so much better!

My brother Andrea Sysyphus for creating such a wonderful cover for this book!

My brother Gary Grindstaff, for always supporting me when I was working on this book.

My NY brother Michael Shatkin, for his endless support and keeping an eye on the Facebook page! A more loyal friend is hard to find!

Germania's Assault Generation

Stefan Willms, my German brother, for his support and for keeping history alive by guiding numerous people through the Hürtgen Forest every year.

Derrick McCormick, my good friend and brother in blue, for always believing in me. I always enjoy our conversations about WWII, German helmets, and German honor daggers.

Oliver Schweinoch of the LEMO (Lebendiges Museum Online) for his help obtaining one of the stories of a Waffen SS veteran.

I would also like to thank the following people for their endless support and believing in me while working on this project: Moritz Loewenstein, Philip O'Brien, Martin Ridgway, Michael Flynn, Gaz Reed, Jim Keeling, Jarred Crump, Axel Van Looy, Lance O. Adams, Kenny Rigaux, Cynthia Mahon, Brett Hankins, JD Clarke, Travis Jacobsen, Al Cameron, John Poole, Jordan Gaiche, Dan McCormack, Andy Van Billemont, Joel Edwards, Michael Falsey, Kim "Auratum" Blok, Jens Box (Bedankt voor den Duvel Kameraad!), Ralf Stinkens (Bedankt voor de medaille!), Robert Zemanko, Angelo Fabbro, Tyler Machalk, John Uys, Kris Kirk, Kraig Jewell, Thomas Mason, Frederick Mclean-Brown, Patrick Krennerich, Karl Redmann, Richie Love, David Walker, John Theisen, Jay Warden, Alan Crook, Gary Hanley, and Gooch.

There are many more people I'd like to thank but then the list of names would be a couple of pages long. My apologies if your name is not here in the list, but know that I'm grateful for your help and support.

Last but not least, a super thank you goes to my wife and kids for their support and patience while I was writing this book. They are the foundation of my existence!

Acknowledgements

Dedicated to:

Rottenführer Martti Lehtonen
FFB/4.Kp.
Finnisches Freiwilligen Bataillon der Waffen SS

Oberscharführer Dries Coolens
Schwerer Granatwerfer Zug
4.Kp./I. Btl/67. Rgt/III. SS-Panzer-Korps

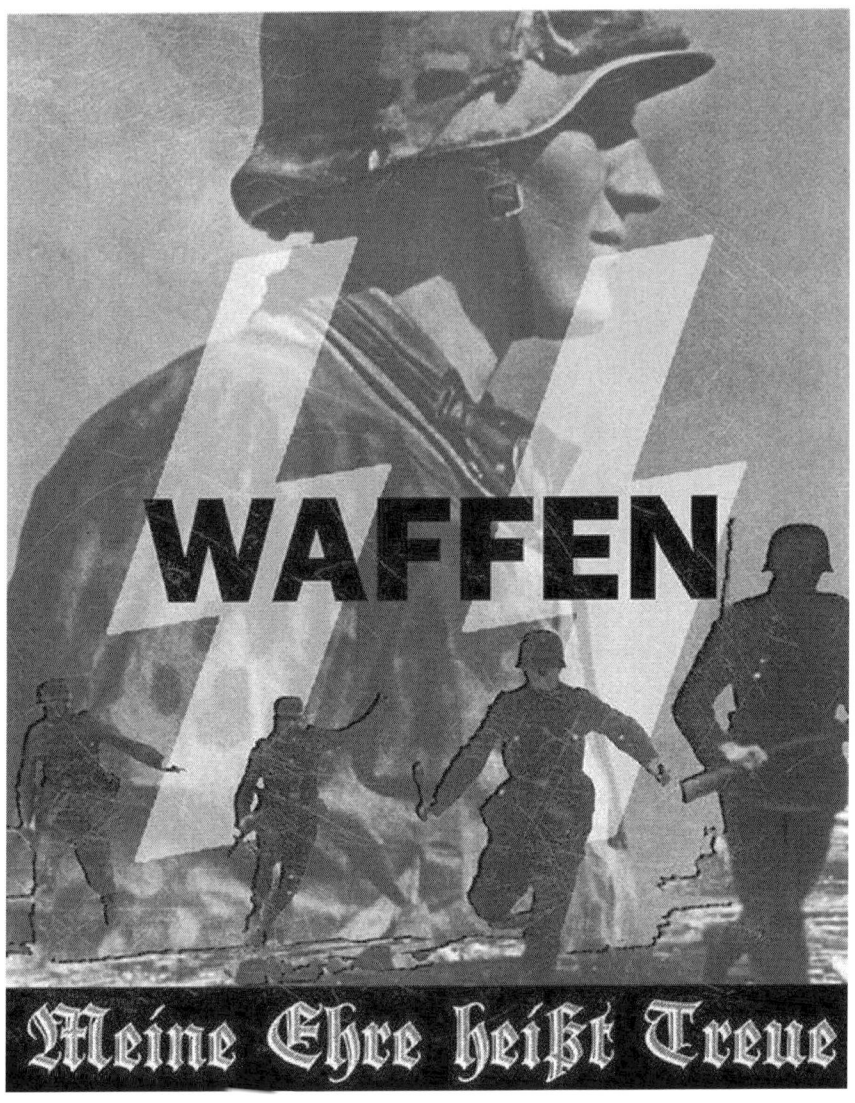

Introduction

The Waffen SS, literally "armed SS", (until 1940, the SS-Verfügungstruppe) is to be distinguished, nominally, from the Allgemeine or General SS. It was a relatively small section of the SS as a whole, created to participate in battles alongside the German Army. Arguments that there was no overlap do not hold: historians have shown a fairly regular exchange of personnel between the two SS organizations. Over the years, 900,000 men served in the Waffen SS. The majority were either citizens of Germany or so-called Volksdeutsche (ethnic Germans), and most of the officers were German. Nonetheless, there was important recruitment from occupied countries. This was a deliberate strategy. According to Heinrich Himmler, a trans-European Waffen SS would form the basis of a "pan-Germanic" and "Nordic" blood community; as such, it was to serve as the birthplace of a future pan-Germanic Europe. Nordic blood, Himmler believed, was not limited to those of German ethnicity. On the contrary, he actively recruited Waffen SS soldiers from all nations thought to share Nordic blood and Germanic heritage. The common experience of service in the Waffen SS would, he hoped, promote the integration of Europe's different "Germanic tribes" into the Greater Germanic Reich. Himmler promoted his Greater Germanic Reich on numerous public occasions, in attempts to concentrate all forces conducive to "Germanic work" within the SS. Indeed, "pan-Germanic idealism" informed official Waffen SS rhetoric throughout the war. The war itself was defined as a trans-European Germanic self-defence against an onslaught by Communists. Or, as Felix Steiner, Commander of the Waffen SS Division Wiking, told his Scandinavian, Flemish, and Dutch volunteers in 1943: "The reason for the war lies in the scorching, culture-destroying, Bolshevist-Asian flood from the East, and the materialistic power of money, which destroys all 'völkischen' and race-specific values, against which are assembled the Germanic elements of order . . . It will take the union of all healthy forces to counter this danger. Thus, the assembly of the Germanic race is an act of self-preservation and necessary self-defence. This could have no better basis than the foundation of the warrior spirit of all Germanic peoples." Within the SS, the "assembly of Nordic blood" and the systematic extermination of Jews, Sinti, Roma, and other "alien peoples" were two sides of the same coin. How, indeed, would it be possible to defend Europe by, for example, conquering and colonizing the "provinces in the East" without increasing the relative numbers of race-conscious Herrenvolk? Himmler quickly arranged for suitable Waffen SS recruitment. In 1940, Waffen SS leaders began to round up volunteers from the "racially related Germanic countries:" Denmark, Norway, Holland, and Flanders. These were then enrolled in two regiments: Westland (for the Flemish and Dutch) and Nordland (Danes and Norwegians). In 1940 – 1941, the two regiments were combined into the 5th Waffen SS Division Wiking. The Division Wiking differed from later foreign-based Waffen SS units (such as, for example, Legion Norge, Legion Niederlande, Freikorps Danmark) in both its mixed national base and its early use in battle. In both senses, it was seen as especially suited to realize Himmler's dream of a pan-Germanic division, the strong foundation stone for a pan-Germanic Europe. The foreign component of "Wiking" volunteers — eventually comprising ten nations — was never larger than 10 per cent of the whole. By the summer of 1941, the division was deep in Soviet territory. It participated in the battle for Rostov-on-Don and the Caucasian oilfields, and was one of the units trapped in the fatal Tsherkassy Pocket (1943 – 1944). Division Wiking's last major engagement, undertaken in the retreat to Austria, was in the Battle for Budapest. Waffen SS veterans are proud of these and similar military campaigns. Their publications and memorial services concentrate on

Introduction

such battles; they were, they maintain, a purely military corps, whose honor precluded any role in war crimes. Wiking's trans-European profile had been useful in promoting Germanic propaganda during the war. After 1945, its supposed European quality proved useful again when trying to argue that the Waffen SS had been unique in not fighting for Germany only, but in defense of all Europe. The Division Wiking's European profile was cited as emblematic of the Waffen SS as a whole: additional proof that Waffen SS veterans were not to be confused with either the Allgemeine SS, or questionable Waffen SS hybrids such as the SS-Totenkopfverbände of the concentration and death camps. In the decades following 1945, veteran groups - so-called Truppenkameradschaften, that is, associations based on former Waffen SS units - and the HIAG, with its monthly journal, "Der Freiwillige" ("The Volunteer"), continued to emphasize this trans-European feature. Der Freiwillige, in particular, rehearsed the history of the Waffen SS, and printed news from veterans throughout Europe, drawing in "European freedom fighters" from Scandinavia, Belgium, Holland, France, and beyond. These efforts did not get it very far. Outside of Germany, Waffen SS veterans were steadfastly ostracized (if not, in the aftermath of defeat, jailed or executed). Eastern European Waffen SS veterans could only organize abroad. German veterans quickly lost ground too when the German media started publicizing SS war crimes. One would think it would be emotionally taxing - if not socially suicidal - to belong to a Waffen SS veterans' association. But veterans' associations meet important needs. These do not necessarily include discussions of the cause of any particular war. Most veterans' associations gloss over their war's justification: veterans fought for freedom, for the Fatherland, and against Communism. The politics that started the war are less important than the subsequent need, felt by many, to remember and maintain connections with war-time comrades, and to reiterate the significance of the sacrifices made by those who fought.

19

Germania's Assault Generation

It is in this context that veterans hope to coordinate and conduct the ritualized and public commemoration of fallen comrades, for their deaths are meaningful only if they are not forgotten. As one soldier stated: "...In seeing death before our eyes, we often realize more clearly the meaning of our existence. Nature is a parable for us. In the middle of winter, everything seems to die and to have bloomed in vain. Yet the falling of the old leaves is necessary for the coming of the new ones, and the falling of the last stalk makes room for the new seeds. Our sacrifice should and will be the source of new strength for our people, whatever sorrow and pain may be involved!" Judging from veterans' association publications, the veterans invest a great deal of time in maintaining relationships with and remembering comrades. Their publications constantly rehearse the most meaningful of their shared experiences - combat - with extensive photographs and texts retelling the history and experience of battalions, battles, victories, and retreats. Veterans' association journals also give much space to present-time camaraderie: anniversaries and celebrations, battlefield tours, and commemorative dinners. Finally, there is the significance of closely related memory work: the honoring of the fallen. This is conducted, for example, by organizing highly ritualized commemorations of the war dead, preferably at some nationally acknowledged public site and, at best, with important speakers, and not least, the enthusiastic support of local populations. But after the war they were considered to be the ultimate traitors/criminals, and their position still remains a difficult element in history. The primary reason for the Waffen SS being condemned as part of a criminal organization was the issue of the Nuremberg court being unable to distinguish between those Waffen SS units that could be called combat units, and those others that had links to the death camps and extermination squads. It would appear that at the time it was easier to issue a blanket ban on all than to attempt to tease out those members/units that had not committed

Introduction

any war crimes or might be deemed to be "only" a combat unit. As the victorious party, the Allies could ultimately decide what they liked, but it did make it very difficult for Waffen SS veterans to support their families after the war. In the logs of the International Military Tribunal, 1946: Vol. 20:370 Paul Hausser answered the question from Herr Pelckmann asking him if he considered that the Waffen SS, in its majority, participated in the crimes which indubitably were committed? Hausser replied: "No. The Prosecution chains the Waffen SS to the fate of Heinrich Himmler and a small circle of criminals around him. The Waffen SS is taking this quite bitterly for it believes that in its majority it fought decently and fairly. It is far removed from these crimes and from the man who is responsible for them. I should like to ask the High Tribunal to please listen to the accounts and the judgments of the front soldiers on your side. I believe that they will not fail to show us respect. Wherever specific incidents occurred they were exceptions. The Waffen SS considers it quite unjust that it is being treated differently from the mass of the German Armed Forces and it does not deserve to be outlawed as a criminal organization." The incidents known in history as massacres and/or other criminal acts are not the result of training, but rather the failure of individuals, perhaps the giving way of nerves when in difficult situations deep in enemy territory. But these accusations for these crimes should not be generalized. Even if there had been 10 instead of only two cases, the ratio as applied to the entire membership of the Waffen SS of one million men would mean there would be one case to every 100,000 men. Such incidents are the results of the intensification of combat on the ground and in a long war; incidents which have occurred on both sides, and will always continue to occur. You cannot hold the bulk of the Waffen SS responsible. Just imagine being at the front. The soldiers settled their helmets more comfortably on their heads and gripped their weapons tighter. This was it. God there were a lot of them out there in the front. But the soldiers knew they had to hold. To hold was to live, to break down was to be torn into bloody shreds in a panic-stricken mob, to be cut to pieces in the dust. Only discipline held them now, that and the proximity of their comrades. After all, running is easy when you're faceless, but when you're surrounded by your neighbors from the street back home, running suddenly becomes the hardest thing to do. If someone ran, everyone would know it and the shame would be tremendous. So, held by fear of failing as much as from discipline, these young men stood their ground and waited with dry throats and bladders suddenly full. The enemy was close now…

The Legionnaires

They called themselves Legionnaires of the Waffen SS, the new European Army. They came from all nations of Europe, and they were wearing the same uniform to fight for the same cause: fighting the strong Russian Armed Forces. Almost one million of these young men fought next to the Wehrmacht during WWII. It was during this era that the ideal of a united Europe was born. There is no other period in history that has been documented like the 6 years that ranged from the invasion of Poland in 1939 to the capitulation in Berlin in 1945. They left their homes, families, and friends with their heart full of joy and pride. They had to endure extreme weather from +40 to -50 while fighting on several fronts. They were battle hardened because of this. They became good soldiers because they knew how to survive in any situation. It's actually mind boggling but at the same time also amazing to think how many young men were prepared to give their lives for Germany and for a better Europe. Even men in their 30s and 40s joined the ranks of the Waffen SS because they wanted to make a change...because they wanted to BE the change. The sad reality is that many of these soldiers never returned back home.

Over the years, more than 900,000 men served in the Waffen SS. One major part of the Waffen SS were either citizens of Germany or so-called Volksdeutsche (ethnic Germans), and most of the officers were German. The other part were foreign volunteers as there was an important recruitment campaign from the occupied countries. This was a deliberate strategy. According to Heinrich Himmler, a trans-European Waffen SS would form the basis of a pan-Germanic and "Nordic" blood community; as such, it was to serve as the birthplace of a future pan-Germanic Europe. Nordic blood, Himmler believed, was not limited to those of German ethnicity. On the contrary, he actively recruited Waffen SS soldiers from all nations thought to share Nordic blood and Germanic heritage. The common experience of service in the Waffen SS would, he hoped, promote the integration of Europe's different Germanic tribes into the Greater Germanic Reich. SS ideology was framed around the notion of this transnational Nordic race and racial community. SS recruitment would not halt at "artificially drawn borders," as the director of the SS-Hauptamt (SS Main Office), Gottlob Berger, put it in a 1944 lecture. Himmler promoted his Greater Germanic Reich on numerous public occasions, in attempts to concentrate all forces conducive to Germanic work within the SS. Indeed, pan-Germanic idealism informed official Waffen SS rhetoric throughout the war. The war itself was defined as a trans-European Germanic self-defense against an onslaught by Communists. Or, as Felix Steiner, Commander of the Waffen SS Division Wiking, told his Scandinavian, Flemish and Dutch volunteers in 1943:

"The reason for the war lies in the scorching, culture-destroying, Bolshevist-Asian flood from the East, and the materialistic power of money, which destroys all "völkischen" and race-specific values, against which are assembled the Germanic elements of order. It will take the union of all healthy forces to counter this danger. Thus, the assembly of the Germanic race is an act of self-preservation and necessary self-defense. This could have no better basis than the foundation of the warrior spirit of all Germanic peoples."

Himmler quickly arranged for suitable Waffen SS recruitment. In 1940, Waffen SS leaders began to round up volunteers from the racially related Germanic countries: Denmark, Norway, Holland, and Flanders (northern Belgium). These were then enrolled in two regiments: Westland (for the Flemish and Dutch) and Nordland (Danes and Norwegians). In 1940 - 1941, the two regiments were combined into the 5th Waffen SS Division Wiking. The Division

The Legionnaires

Wiking differed from later foreign-based Waffen SS units (such as, for example, Legion Norge, Legion Niederlande, Freikorps Danmark) in both its mixed national base and its early use in battle. In both senses, it was seen as especially suited to realize Himmler's dream of a pan-Germanic division, the strong cornerstone of a pan-Germanic Europe.

Every man of this almost one million strong fighting force, whether he'd be missing in action, killed in action, or still alive, has a personal story to tell; this war still has a lot of stories to tell. Most of these stories of Waffen SS soldiers were kept secret and were only told to a few people while speaking with a silent voice. What you're about to read are stories of Waffen SS soldiers that left their families and friends behind to go to war. Fortunately some of them made it back, and their stories are an exploration of their determination, their morality, their courage, and their identity. At a certain point in one's existence, one comes to get aligned with that part to be able to understand what happened. There are certain mysteries from the past that we'd like to explore. Sometimes these were human dramas, dramas who were the consequences of war, of a conflict - sometimes personal conflicts. It is then that we start doing research with what's available at that moment.

When Germany occupied the majority of Europe, there was a certain group of young men that decided to sign up for this new army called the Waffen SS. June 1941: Hitler launches Operation Barbarossa and invades the Soviet Union. Hitler's crusade against Communism had started. Everywhere in Europe, collaborating states/regimes started providing men, most of them devoted Christians, for the Führer's crusade. Their departure to the front to an unknown future was a moving event for their family and friends. There was such an enthusiasm, courage, and strength when they departed on the trains to the front. It was their beliefs and their pride that motivated them, and with this motivation they were able to move mountains. History has condemned these young men as crusaders. They see them as the old crusaders that left for Jerusalem to fight for the Catholic faith. However how can one condemn a young man of 17 years of age who left school to risk his life? Can you imagine how it could be possible that at this age one was prepared to sacrifice everything he had?

When these European volunteers enlisted, they were all shipped to Germany where they would receive the same uniform and training as their German brothers-in-arms. The first taste of life as a soldier came in the barracks far away from home. It was during special ceremonies in those training camps that these young men would swear allegiance to the German Army and the Führer. However their loyalty was first and foremost towards the legion they belonged to and their leaders. Real life as a soldier started right there and military discipline and weapons training was of great importance. Then came the front: the "Vormarsch" or pre-marsh of hundreds of kilometers towards the front lines to confront the enemy armies on their own soil. While marching to the front something interesting occurred when these divisions were passing through cities and towns. The welcome they received from the local population was heartwarming. Multiple Walloon Legionnaires had interactions with the locals in Russia, and of course the Belgian flag on their uniform drew the attention of the people. In Russia the people had never heard of Belgium before, and when these Legionnaires were asked what they were going to do they replied, "We come to fight Bolshevism!" The answer from the local population was stunning and came like a shock: "We've been waiting for you for a long time!" The welcome these Legionnaires received was almost surreal. They were given food, shelter, and they were treated as liberators. They liberated the people from a long ongoing nightmare they were living in for years

The Legionnaires

prior to their arrival. The people were free now thanks to these foreign soldiers. For these soldiers there were no politics involved, but they were all condemned as criminals after the war.

The long marches to the front were not always easy as the equipment they had to carry felt like lead under the burning sun. Once in a while, time was taken to write a letter home which was thousands of kilometers away. But also receiving mail and packages from home was a joyful moment in a soldier's life. Once they arrived at the front, life wasn't as easy as one would think it would be. On the contrary, it was a daily struggle to survive in the hope to gain some terrain on the enemy forces. Life and death were so close to each other, and many men lost their lives during the campaign. Stalingrad was the first major defeat of the Wehrmacht during WWII, but certain people, like Leon Degrelle for example, took advantage of that defeat to show that foreign legions would be very useful for the German Army. The ultimate goal was to become indispensable to the German high command. The reputation of his legion reassured his success and it was then that his legion was incorporated into the Waffen SS. For many people these two letters "SS" bring back memories of camps and maltreatment of prisoners…memories about genocide, but the main difference between the Waffen SS and camp guards is often ignored.

Between December 1943 and February 1944 during the Russian advance to the West, about 60,000 German soldiers found themselves surrounded in the Korsun-Cherkasy pocket in the Ukraine. The risk here was that the troops could get completely isolated from the rest of the world. The Germans had to face tens of thousands of Russian troops, and it became a bitter fight which knew no mercy at all. The Waffen SS in Korsun, Degrelle in particular (after SS-Sturmbannführer Lucien Lippert was killed), was tasked to hold the lines to keep a path open for the rest of the German troops to safely retreat from this hellhole. The Waffen SS troops stood their ground even if they were outnumbered 6 to 1 and suffering heavy losses. But they succeeded, and they kept the way open which saved a significant number of lives by sacrificing their own. That day, the Waffen SS, and the Walloons in particular, were the heroes of the day and it was after that battle that Degrelle was summoned to Berlin to receive the Knight's Cross from Hitler himself. It was back then that Leon Degrelle reached his objective.

On June 6, 1944, the inevitable happened and the Allies landed on the beaches in Normandy. The armies of the free world were now en route to liberate France, Belgium, and many other countries on their way to Germany. It was also then that the Communist resistance started a campaign of terror in the occupied territories. The German authorities in these occupied territories reacted by performing executions and many times this involved innocent civilians. Many of the Waffen SS troops - most of them were foreign volunteers - who were still in the occupied territories were sent back to Germany to regroup and get reinforcements. The following months were very hard for these Waffen SS soldiers, knowing that the situation they were in wasn't favorable at all: the Allies and the Russians were advancing on all fronts, and the soldiers already knew that the end was near.

In January 1945, a major Russian offensive started on the Vistula River, attacking the German positions in the Warsaw area. The Russian armored units penetrated Poland, and came to a stop at the Oder River. The German Armies were in full retreat and multiple divisions were now surrounded by enemy forces. Thousands of refugees from the war torn areas were fleeing the advancing Russian hordes, and were at the same time blocking the roads for the German forces. By the end of January 1945, the Walloon and Langemarck Divisions were given the order to make their way to the front in the

The Legionnaires

East. They were put on trains with all their equipment, but the final destination was unknown. The German forces were fighting on so many fronts that it was sometimes unclear where a soldier had to go and fight! The divisions arrived in the area of Stettin and Stargard in early February. The weather was not in their favor at all: it was cold and raining. Besides the bad weather, the military situation wasn't favorable either as it gained catastrophic proportions. Leon Degrelle's men of the 69th Regiment of the 28.SS-Freiwilligen-Panzergrenadier-Division "Wallonien" fiercely defended their positions nearly until the last man. In Degrelle's after action report of February 18, 1945, he wrote in the French language:

"Report of SS-Obersturmbannführer Leon Degrelle, commander of the 28.SS-Freiw. Gren. Div. 'Wallonien'"

This is the report about 51 Walloon volunteers who sacrificed themselves during a man-to-man close combat battle which lasted 27 hours to protect and secure the South-East flank of the SS-Polizei-Division during the offensive in southern Pomerania. During the night of February 14 - 15, the SS-Division "Wallonien" received the orders to secure the route Stargard-Repplin onto which on February 16 the SS-Polizei-Division had to make its advance to launch the attack direction south.

The 69th Walloon Regiment's mission was:

1) To annex the village of Leopoldsruh and hold ground cost what cost. In the morning on February 15 the 1st Battalion of the 69th Walloon Regiment annexed Leopoldsruh after repressing the Soviet Infantry who was defending their positions with a strength of 200 men.

2) To annex the crests of Lindenberg to the South-East of Krussow after crossing the River Ina.

Lindenberg (Lipnik)

The annexation and occupation of Lindenberg was from great importance because it allowed to maintain the fortified Russian positions and communications under constant fire, against whom, for two days and two nights the powerful counter-attacks of tanks and infantry of the Reich had fought a major battle. This strategic position of Lindenberg was formed by a long clay cliff which was somewhat elevated and isolated in the midst of a vast marshy flat plain without any trees. Only two small fir trees extended the cliff to the marshes which stretched to the south-east in the direction of the locality of Kolin. It was from Kolin that an attack was launched by the 7th Company and one platoon of heavy weapons of the 8th Company of the 2nd Battalion of the 69th Walloon Regiment. They succeeded by reaching the two fir trees thanks to the promptness of the Walloon combat system. They threw down the enemy and after a quick man-to-man fight they conquered the cliffs of Lindenberg. It was 1150h. A second operation took place after a violent engagement in Gut Karlsburg which was situated at the edge of Lindenberg, between Lindenberg and the locality of Strebelow (Strzeblewo), where until then the HKL or Hauptkampflinie was situated. Thus in two stages the protection of the Vormarsch planned for the following day was assured and the communications of the enemy towards the Bolshevik base in Krussow was blocked by our artillery.

Enemy Counter-Attack

The enemy quickly realized in what danger its base in Krussow was from where it had established its offensive system in direction of Stargard. The Walloons' mission was to maintain their positions for 24 hours. The objective was to be clinched to the ground in the early morning on February 16 when the great German armored attack would be initiated from Repplin direction south. When the battle began the Russians quickly figured out the "Lindenberg" maneuver and promptly they brought five tanks and one infantry battalion in position. The Walloons hadn't any support left from the German artillery who was already following the tanks nor did they have support from any PAK units. It was only with their Panzerfaust and personal weapons that they were supporting this terrible battle. A Russian tank was hit hard by a Panzerfaust and completely destroyed. All the Russians inside the tank were killed one after the other when they tried to escape the tank. The other Russian tanks, obviously more careful this time, kept out of range of our Panzerfaust. Their turrets were just coming over the crest of the cliff firing on our positions one at the time. It was then that a young Walloon officer, Lt Poels, already hit by 4 bullets in the abdomen and shoulder, instead of having him evacuated from the terrain, decided to cross the terrain armed with a Panzerfaust. He wanted to close the distance so he could incinerate one of the tanks. He was killed during his heroic attempt. The quick defense of the Walloons was so fierce that the Russian infantry had, despite it unleashed 3 attacks, to give up some terrain. Also their tanks were retreating for a couple of 100 meters. Unfortunately the Walloon losses were extremely high and ammunition was running low.

Reinforcements

The 69th Regiment did the impossible to rescue the defenders of Lindenberg but a Russian tank had itself positioned on the South-East of Lindenberg. It swept the terrain every time we tried to approach it. From an entire platoon which was progressing under the tank's heavy fire only 8 men under the command of Lt Jourdain succeeded to enter the cliff. The Lieutenant himself was hit by a bullet in his leg.

A New Soviet Attack

At 1430h the four remaining - and intact - tanks, reinforced by 2 new tanks joined the attack again with the help of hundreds of assailants of a Soviet Battalion. Again the tanks stayed out of reach of our Panzerfausts and every attempt to get closer to them on the uncovered terrain was swept away the enemy infantry's Maxim machine guns. However thanks to the fanaticism of several volunteers a second tank was hit in the turret. But the volleys of the other tanks crushed the teams of the defenders. This would allow the Soviet Battalions to take our positions one by one. The Walloons defended their positions with such an energy and passion that more than 80 Russians were killed during this man-to-man battle. Our men allowed themselves to be butchered there. We could hear the crying and screaming from our wounded who were killed by the bayonets of the assailants. The command post of first Lieutenant Cappelle, a splendid young officer, who was surrounded with the last survivors, were desperately defending their positions meter by meter. During this period 19 severely wounded covered by this last nest of resistance were dragging themselves towards Kolin while the bullets were flying over them. At 1630h it was the end. The few survivors only had a few dozen cartridges left. They would throw themselves back onto the enemy. When he saw clearly that in spite of his wounds he was going to fall into the hands of the Soviet troops, first Lieutenant Cappelle got back on his feet in between the millions of dead soldiers; he ran straight ahead and at a couple of meters away from the enemy, with his last cartridge in his pistol, he shot his brains out. From the 81 Walloons who during a hallucinating 27 hours of man-to-man combat, and who defended that cliff, only 8 were able to reach Kolin during the night. From the other 73 men 19 were severely wounded and were able to be evacuated just in time; 3 were captured by the enemy. The other 51, officers included, were all dead heroes who had fiercely defended their positions. The information of the last resistance was provided by Lieutenant Lovinfosse who was wounded four times (one bullet in the neck, one in the chest, one in his head, and one in his hand). By playing dead and by going through 1.25m of water and marshland he was able to join our lines during the night. He still had the strength to state the orders to maintain the positions for 24 hours. We maintained our positions for 27 hours; mission accomplished!

This is how 51 Walloons sacrificed themselves protecting the flanks the entire time of the tanks that were traveling on the road of liberation through southern Pomerania."

The Legionnaires

The last bridgeheads in Pomerania were abandoned by the end of March. General Heinrici who was considered one of the best tacticians of WWII knew that a Russian breakthrough at the Oder River was inevitable. He therefore left a handful of troops at the Oder Front. Heinrici preferred to organize a mobile resistance in the background with the armored vehicles that were still at his disposal.

The Russian attack was of such magnitude that both sides suffered an enormous amount of casualties. The Oder River was the last natural border before entering Germany. General Batov of the 65th Army said that the Oder River was the equivalent of two times the Dnieper River, and one time the Vistula River. They knew that the Oder River was very hard to cross because in this area the river split in two parts: the eastern arm which was called the "Große Ringes", and the western arm which was called the Western Oder. Instead of only crossing one river, the Russians had to cross two! Another factor that had to be calculated into the Russian battle plan was that the area around and in between the Oder River arms was a swampy area which couldn't be crossed by heavy equipment. Only the infantry could make their advance; they had to cross the river with boats and take the land on the other side before they could start building bridges. Not an easy task, but on April 16 the Russians started their offensive on the Oder River. The Russian infantry had already crossed the Oder in small groups. This location in Pomerania was one of the crucial points towards the final battle in Berlin. The Russians tried to cross the Oder on the north and the south side of the freeway bridge, and in the area of Schillersdorf. It took them a couple of hours however, because they were able to hold their positions, the Germans were unable to push them back and recover some of the lost territory. More and more Russian troops started to come into the area...

Germania's Assault Generation

On April 20, 1945, on Hitler's birthday, a destructive artillery barrage had started on the German defense lines. The magnitude of this destructive artillery bombing had such a magnitude that it looked almost inhuman! The Russians had placed more than 238 pieces of artillery in an area of only 1 km of length. This means that there was a piece of artillery placed at every 4 meters along that 1 km stretch! Multiple Russian bridgeheads were established on a 5 km front between Kurow and Schillersdorf. The German counterattacks were futile, and the Russians were able to fortify their positions on the left bank of the Oder River. SS Obersturmbannführer Konrad Schellong who was in command of the German troops at the Oder Front only had three battalions at his disposition: a Flemish Battalion on the left flank, the Pomeranian Battalion Kohlberg on the right flank, and in the middle, the Walloon Battalion of Derriks. The Germans ordered the counterattack, and between April 21-22 the attacks continued on the Russian positions in the Schillersdorf area. The Russians became stronger every day, however, but they didn't advance as much as they initially had hoped. Maybe 100 to 200 meters. The Walloons were given the order to keep on pushing forward as they were deemed to be the strongest and most battle hardened battalion. But the mission for the Walloons was of a tragic simplicity. They had to establish their positions in the dunes near the Oder River and attack the advancing Russian infantry near Schillersdorf. The Russian offensives were of such violence, and the fighting for Schillersdorf, the man-to-man assaults, took many lives from both sides. It was when the German armored vehicles almost ran out of ammunition that Major Hellebaut, commander of the Flemish and Walloon forces, ordered a retreat. The Russians wanted to reach Berlin no matter what. It was a race against the Allies who were getting closer to Germany on the Western Front. With the Russians getting closer to Berlin, the Germans knew that this would mean the end. Troops were gathered to fight the final battles, and units that were familiar with the local

The Legionnaires

areas were put on the front lines as they knew all the positions of bunker, trenches, etc. However it was a very difficult task for the German Army as they ran out of resources: it was near the end of the war and most equipment, ammo, and most importantly, the manpower was almost gone.

At the Oder River, the defense lines were built and the men prepared to hold back the Russians to reassure a safe retreat for the rest of German troops. But there was always the danger of a surprise attack from the enemy forces, so one needed to be vigilant all the time. Both sides knew the end was near: the Russians wanted to attack for the last time and spearhead to Berlin, while the Germans, knowing that it was too late, wanted to hold their positions at all costs. The majority of the German soldiers knew it was useless to keep on fighting, but for the Waffen SS it was one more day of freedom. Most of the Waffen SS volunteers, especially the foreign volunteers, knew that they were going to be killed or sentenced to death in their homelands or imprisoned for a long time. Hence the reason they kept on fighting.

On April 23, 1945, the Russian infantry advanced towards the German positions, however there was something that wasn't right. It was too calm. Was this an ambush? Suddenly the first shots were fired and the first casualties fell. In the meantime, one could hear the rumbling of the engines in the far distance from the approaching tanks while the artillery started firing at will. All hell broke loose and the Russians opened fire from all directions. The T-34 tank was a fierce enemy tank, some even call it the best tank on the Eastern Front, and it was feared by many German soldiers. During this firestorm, the men of the Waffen SS were able to hold their positions for a while. Equipped with Panzerfaust, Panzerschrecks, and MG42s, they fought the advancing Russian Army. But the fighting would be over soon as the German command post surrendered, making it possible for the Russians to take all strategic points to enter northern Germany and to end the fighting there. The Russians were everywhere now, and they continued their advance to Berlin which would soon become a front city or "Frontstadt".

Walloon volunteers in Pomerania - 1945.

Rottenführer Martti Lehtonen – FFB/4.kp – Finnisches Freiwilligen Bataillon der Waffen SS/4. Kp.

SS-ROTTENFÜHRER MARTTI LEHTONEN – FINNISH VOLUNTEER

This is the story told by Martti Lehtonen's granddaughter Jaana Lehtonen. This is also a chronicle of one Finnish soldier and his comrades serving in the ranks of the Waffen SS. Jaana never met her grandfather Martti Lehtonen because he died in 1961, ten years before Jaana Lehtonen was born. It was in 1999 when Jaana became interested in her grandfather's past and especially about his service in the Waffen SS. Over the years, Jaana researched information about her grandfather, interviewed relatives, and the other Finnish men that served in the same battalion as Martti during his time in with the 5. SS-Division Wiking. Martti also kept a diary for a short period of time during the war, and his relatives also had kept some letters that he had sent from the front lines. Jaana also managed to get some copies of Martti's comrades' unpublished memoirs. It's because of her passion for the history of her grandfather and her nation that the memory of Martti will stay alive forever.

Martti's Childhood and Youth - Rough Beginnings

Europe was in chaos as the waves of WWI swept across the continent. The Russian Empire was collapsing, and in the East, the Grand Duchy of Finland was leaning towards separation from the empire. In 1918, Finland was taking its first steps as a nation when Martti "Napsu" Lehtonen was born. The government of Finland had declared its independence on December 6, 1917, and in January 1918 a short but bloody civil war broke out between senate led forces (Whites) and the rebel forces led by Socialists (Reds). The civil war ended in a victory for the Whites on May 15, 1918. Martti Kalervo Lehtonen was born just one month later on June 15, 1918 in Hausjärvi. Hausjärvi is a small town about 100 km north of the capital Helsinki. During that spring, the local Red troops tried to recruit Martti's father to join the fight, but he refused. Martti was the youngest of three children: the oldest was his brother Urho who was 6 years older, and his sister Aino who was 4 years older.

Times were rough for the newly formed nation and for Martti's family. His father died when Martti was still a baby and just to make the situation even worse, his mother was unemployed. They moved to the western coast of Finland to a city called Pori. Martti's aunts were living in Pori and that provided some support for the difficult situation they were in. The move didn't solve all the problems at once, and the family's situation was so bad that Martti and his brother Urho were sent to a foster home for a period of time because their mother couldn't afford to provide for a living for her children. The time in the foster home was harsh for Martti and Urho. There wasn't enough food or clothes and the rules in the foster home were very strict. But it wasn't all bad for Martti. He found joy in many hobbies like swimming and shooting for example. Martti was a good shooter and he won quite many trophies. Many of these trophies were used in yard games and some of them got lost over the years.

As the years went by, things got better for his family. After his school years, Martti got a job in a machinery workshop. At the age of 19 it was his turn for military service in the Finnish Army. From its beginnings, the Finnish Army has been a conscript army. Every man had to enlist the year he turned 18. During that time, one had to go through several medical examinations after which it was decided into which particular unit a conscript would be placed. Martti's call-up was on September 6, 1938. He was accepted for and he was placed into a field artillery regiment. On January 4, 1938 Martti joined the

Rottenführer Martti Lehtonen – FFB/4.kp – Finnisches Freiwilligen Bataillon der Waffen SS/4. Kp.

Field Artillery Regiment 1 (Finnish: Kenttätykistörykmentti 1, KTR 1) which was the beginning of his almost continuous five years of military service. Little did he know what kind of struggles he and the whole country were about to face...

Winter War – First Call to Arms

The situation in Europe was going from one diplomatic crisis into another in the 1930s. The whole western world was shocked when Stalin and Hitler found ways of co-operation between their nations by establishing the so called "Molotov-Ribbentrop Pact" which was signed on August 23, 1939 (also known as the "German-Russian Non-Aggression Pact"). This pact also included a secret protocol in which Stalin and Hitler had divided territories of Poland, the Baltic States, Romania, and Finland. These secret protocols sealed the faith of Finland immediately, and it was in the spring of 1938 that Russian diplomats and NKVD agents already had informed Finland's foreign minister about the lack of trust that Russia had for the Finnish government. After the Molotov-Ribbentrop Pact was signed, the pressure from the Russian side began to grow. A Finnish delegation was invited to Moscow in October, 1939 for negotiations. The Finnish delegations and their Russian counterparts had three meetings between October 12 and November 9, but both sides were unable to find an agreement of any kind. The Russian Army had already started its preparations for the invasion in September, 1939, so these negotiations were just political masquerade. The mobilization of the Finnish forces started in October, 1939 which also resulted in Martti's artillery regiment receiving its orders and starting the march towards the eastern border with Russia.

On November 30, 1939, Russian forces began the invasion of Finland. The Russian Army attacked with 21 divisions (almost 500,000 men) against a poorly equipped Finnish Army which was just over 250,000 men strong. The Finnish Army didn't even have enough material for the troops. There was a terrible lack of clothes, weapons, and ammunitions. This first war, which was called the "Winter War", lasted 105 days. Martti fought during the entire duration of the war. He fought in the battles of Leipäsuo, Kämärä, and Karisalmi. The cease-fire took effect on March 13, 1939. The peace treaty was signed the day before in Moscow. Finland lost the Karelia region (this included the second largest city at the time: Vyborg (Finnish: Viipuri). The Finnish Army marched to the newly drawn border and the disbanding of the field army had begun. Martti remained in the army to complete his military service, and he was discharged on July 6, 1940. After the peace treaty was signed, things started to turn in Europe. The war ended but the relations between Russia and Finland never returned to normal. Finland was still settling things with Russia when the rumor began that this peace wasn't going to last for long.

Between a Rock and a Hard Place - Finland in 1940-1941: The Political Background That Led to the Continuation War

As earlier said, there wasn't much help for Finland during the Winter War. Finland received lots of sympathy from the other European nations but it was left all alone to fight the war against the Russian aggressor. Germany had to honor the Molotov-Ribbentrop Pact, and all material and weapons transports that were shipped via Germany to Finland were halted. Germany's foreign policy towards Finland was that Finland should accept the terms that the Soviet Union had presented. In the 1930s, Fascists and nationalist movements were gaining support in various countries across Europe, but this wasn't the case in Finland. It was after the Civil War that various nationalist movements and far right parties had their peak in Finnish politics in the 1920s. The success of those movements rapidly declined, and in 1930 the social democratic party won the

Rottenführer Martti Lehtonen – FFB/4.kp – Finnisches Freiwilligen Bataillon der Waffen SS/4. Kp.

elections (but the government stayed in the hands of the centrist parties). So viewing this background, Finland's efforts to steer their foreign policy towards Scandinavian countries and Great Britain seemed logical. At the time, Germany wasn't seen as an ally that supported Finland's efforts of being a neutral country in northern Europe. Germany offered Finland a non-aggression treaty in 1939, but the Finnish government declined the offer. After the Winter War and after the events that had happened in Europe at the same time, something changed in the German-Finnish relationship.

Parade in Finland.

Russian forces had occupied the Baltic States in 1940, and there was a growing pressure towards Finland. Finnish communists got their orders from Moscow, and they organized under the name of the Finnish-Soviet Friendship Association. This group managed to cause several riots and protests in Finland. Also, a Finnish passenger plane named Kaleva (Junker Ju 52) was shot down in June 1940. The plane was flying from Tallinn (Estonia) to Helsinki when a Red Army fighter, without warning, opened fire. The Finnish government and newspapers tried to hide this event from the public, and no government complaint was sent to the Russian diplomats or officials. The fear of a Russian reaction was so strong that it seemed better to remain silent. There was also another crisis in Finland known as the "nickel crisis". Finland had a nickel mine in Petsamo (located in the north, on the shores of the Arctic Ocean). Russia tried to take control of that mine which led to another diplomatic crisis.

In this situation, Germany's attitude towards Finland started to change. Trade relationships were established in the summer of 1940 and in August, after the negotiations, Finland granted transit rights to German troops. Germany needed a safe path to supply their troops in Norway. Because of this arrangement, Finland agreed on reasonable terms to buy weapons from Germany. In November 1940, the Russian foreign minister Molotov visited Hitler and one of topics of the talks was Finland. Molotov wanted to finish what they had started during the Winter War. In Finland the government didn't know anything about Molotov's demands, and there were only some rumors. Finland was completely isolated as Germany ruled the Baltic area and all possible western allies were cut off. It was a hard reality for Finland and because it needed protection against a possible aggressor, all of this led to a closer relationship with Germany.

It was in the beginning of 1941 when the first rumors started spreading about an upcoming German invasion of Russia. In January, Generaloberst Halder (Chief of the General Staff of the Army, OKH) mentioned to the Finnish General Heinrichs that Germany had plans of an offensive against Russia and that they might be starting actions in June. General Heinrichs kept this matter only in small circles of trusted people which also included President Risto Ryti, Minister of Trade Väinö Tanner, and the Commander-in-chief of the Finnish Army Field Marshal Mannerheim. This was the "unofficial war cabinet" of the Finnish government. The events started to escalate quite rapidly after this and with the information

Rottenführer Martti Lehtonen – FFB/4.kp – Finnisches Freiwilligen Bataillon der Waffen SS/4. Kp.

about a possible German invasion of Russia, it was decided that now might be the time to get compensation for the losses during the Winter War. It was in March when the initiative of enlisting Finnish men into the Waffen SS was presented to the Finnish officials. In May it was tentatively decided that Finland would take part in the German campaign against Russia, and the final decision was made in early June.

Recruitment of the Finnish Battalion

The request for the recruitment of Finnish men was accepted in March, and after that SS-Standartenführer Dahm came to Finland to organize the recruitment. Dahm already had similar experience as he had been in charge of the recruiting in Holland and in Norway. The Finnish Foreign Ministry was opposed to the fact that Dahm was responsible for the recruiting, as in his perspective it was Finland's own matter to carry out the recruitment. At the same time, it was also decided that recruitment would be done secretly and this is how it was done. In other countries, the Waffen SS was recruiting men publicly. There were also other conditions and terms asked by the Finnish government. One was that the recruited men would serve in the Wehrmacht and not in Waffen SS. The Germans obviously didn't accept this. It was also made clear that all the Finnish men should be in one unit together, and that they weren't going to serve with other men from the other German occupied countries. This term wasn't followed at all once the war started. The contract period for the new recruits was settled for two years.

The former head of the Finnish secret police, Esko Riekki, was put in charge of recruitment. As mentioned earlier, this whole recruitment was kept secret and only trustworthy people were engaged to assist in this process. The Finnish Home Guard, which was a voluntary militia, was also used in the recruitment process, although on an unofficial basis. The aim was to recruit healthy young men out of every social class. To the annoyance of Waffen SS officials, Riekki willfully made the decision that members of right-wing movements were not to be accepted. Of course it was impossible to rule them all out and it has been estimated that only fewer than 20% (approx. 173 men out of 1400) of the battalion's strength were members of right-wing parties or had some kind of connection to these movements. Over 1900 applications were received from all over the country and 1200 of those were accepted. The second phase in the recruitment process was carried out in autumn 1942 to form a Reserve Company (200 men in total). In 1941, all recruits traveled to Helsinki where they were interviewed and medically examined. The recruits had put up a cover story to hide the real purpose of the recruitment: they said that they were going to be workers and that they were going to be seconded to Germany for work. The newly recruited men were shipped to Germany in five batches between May 6 and June 5, 1941.

Martti's Recruitment

As Martti was discharged from the Finnish Army in July 1940, he went back to Pori to continue his life there. Martti was a member of the Home Guard and most likely that is the source of Martti's information about the recruitment for the Waffen SS. In Pori, the recruiters were mainly members of the Home Guard. Martti was also one of the best marksmen in the Guard, and he was well known for his patriotism. These might be the reasons why the recruiters approached him immediately.

Martti was very enthusiastic about this new opportunity. Obviously like in many similar stories through history, the mothers didn't always share their son's decisions. This was also the case when Martti told his mother about his intentions to join the ranks of

Rottenführer Martti Lehtonen – FFB/4.kp – Finnisches Freiwilligen Bataillon der Waffen SS/4. Kp.

German Army. His mother was strongly against it, and his brother Urho also criticized and questioned the whole thing. Martti tried to explain that he was only going to Germany to get decent military training since the German Army was thought to be one of the best armies in the world. Despite his family's protests, Martti sent in his application for the Waffen SS.

In May 1941, recruiters in Pori had collected 70 applications. It was May 20 when Martti and 24 other men took a night train from Pori to Helsinki. In Helsinki, the medical examinations were held in the Ostrobothnia Student Nation's house. After the physical, all men were sent back home where they had to wait for further orders. Soon the orders came, and Martti was in the fourth contingent of men that was shipped on June 2, 1941 to Germany.

Shipment to Germany: Becoming a Soldier in the 5. SS-Division Wiking

Just like the first three contingents, the men of the fourth contingent also gathered in Helsinki. Like all the others from this contingent, Martti had received orders to arrive in Helsinki on May 29. There the men were divided in platoons. Small festivities were arranged in the Ostrobothnia Student Nation's house for the men that were leaving for Germany. On the evening of June 1, the men gathered in small groups and walked to the Helsinki railway station where they took the night train to Vaasa. It was a normal passenger train, not a military train, with the exception that there were three cars added to the back which were reserved for the recruits only. The next morning the train arrived at the harbor of Vaasa.

Moored at the quay was the steam ship Bahia Laura. It was a 12,000 dwt cargo ship that Germans had seized from the English during WWI. Two months, later the Bahia Laura was torpedoed and sunk off the coast of Norway by the Royal Navy submarine HMS

Germania's Assault Generation

Trident on August 30, 1941. Men embarked, and the voyage to Germany began in the afternoon around 1415h when the Bahia Laura sailed into the open sea. Luckily they didn't face any storms but strong winds and a bit of waves caused some seasickness on board, especially among the men who were not use to traveling by ship. After three days at sea, the Bahia Laura arrived at the coast of Poland and sailed past Swinemünde (*Świnoujście*, in Polish) on the morning of June 5. All the men were admiring the Kriegmarine's battleships that were moored in the harbor of Swinemünde. From Swinemünde, they continued to sail to the harbor of Stettin (*Szczecin*, in Polish) were they arrived around noon.

All the men were loaded off the ship, and lunch was served in the harbor. The soup that was served for lunch became famous among these men and it was given the nickname "Stettin Soup." After lunch they had to march to the nearby train station where a train was waiting. From Stettin the train travelled to Stralsund. The train arrived in Stralsund in the evening, and from the train station men marched to the SS barracks located about 2 km from the station. The barracks didn't look like army barracks; they looked rather like old mansions. Even though the buildings were looking good, the accommodations had a lack of decent beds and other conveniences. There were only straw filled mattresses and wooden bunks, but at that time they were good enough for these tired men. But Martti wasn't as tired, and together with a couple of other volunteers went they went AWOL (absence without official leave). They managed to get some drinks and came back to the barracks pretty drunk. This was something that Martti and his comrades would never forget!

The next three days (June 6-8) were used for medical examinations and fitting of the uniforms and other equipment. Some sold their civilian clothes to the local people after they received their uniforms. Identifications tags and service books were also distributed.

Rottenführer Martti Lehtonen – FFB/4.kp – Finnisches Freiwilligen Bataillon der Waffen SS/4. Kp.

On June 8 the last equipment check-ups were done, and the next morning they had to board a train with a destination of Vienna, Austria. It took three days to get there. The train traveled through Berlin (staying overnight there), Dresden, and Prague. In every train station, there were numerous trains packed with soldiers and the Finnish recruits were all wondering why all these trains were there. The traffic on the railways was very busy, but at that time they didn't know that these were the actual preparations for Operation Barbarossa and that the deployment of German forces to the eastern borders had started.

It was a hot summer day when they arrived in Vienna and the men had to wait for almost two hours dressed in full gear at the station before they began the 10 km march to the barracks. The men were hungry and some men passed out during the march because of dehydration and exhaustion. The barracks were located in Schönbrunn, and after the men were settled in, a meal was served. They were also informed that from now on their ranks would be SS-Anwärter, regardless of one's previous military rank prior to joining the Waffen SS!

Training and Formation of the Finnish Battalion

On June 15, 1941, "SS-Freiwilligen Bataillon Nord-Ost" was officially established. The fifth batch of new recruits arrived on June 17, and the battalion had its full four companies completed on June 18. All the battalions' officers and NCOs were German. Hauptsturmführer Hans Collani was appointed the battalion's commander. Hauptsturmführer Hans Collani (February 13, 1908, Szczecin - July 29, 1944, Narva) was the son of a Pomeranian officer: his father having been an infantry Colonel. Before Hans Collani joined the army, he was a sailor in Germany's merchant fleet. In 1932, he joined the NSDAP and the Sturmabteilung (SA), after which he joined the Leibstandarte Adolf Hitler. Collani became one of the company commanders in that new SS unit. He also served as an adjutant of SS-Gruppenführer (rank in 1933) Josef "Sepp" Dietrich. Hans Collani also served in this unit during the invasion of Poland and France. Following these battles, he served in the staff of the SS-Regiment Nordland and the SS-Division Wiking until he was appointed as the new commander of the newly established battalion of Finnish volunteers.

Martti was ordered to serve in the battalion's 4th Company (heavy company). The commander of this company was SS-Obersturmführer Franz Pleiner. Their training started with very basic military skills: how to stand at attention, handling of a rifle, marching, and other basic infantry skills. The training also consisted of a lot of classroom courses. Men were studying the German language (during the recruitment there was no requirements of language skills), military terms, and weapon techniques, ranks, and even singing lessons. The day started very early in the morning and lasted to late in the evening. Everything was done with strict Prussian discipline which was very hard. Martti wasn't quite pleased about how things went in basic training. Keep in mind that he was a battle hardened veteran who had completed military training in the Finnish Army who had fought during the Winter War. Maybe the German military practice wasn't the way that Martti was used to doing things in the Finnish Army. Obviously he had his fair share of problems with the drill instructors. One day the company was training in the barracks yard. The men were ordered to crawl over the terrain and the exercise was repeated over and over again. The drill instructor came and kicked Martti's feet because his boots weren't close enough to the ground. Martti gave a bad stare to the drill instructor, took his rifle, and then started to chase the drill instructor. The German NCO got away, but Martti got his punishment for his actions. One of Martti's comrades said

Rottenführer Martti Lehtonen – FFB/4.kp – Finnisches Freiwilligen Bataillon der Waffen SS/4. Kp.

after the war that during basic training, he and Martti had been punished once again for some misdemeanor and they had to do running exercises with their rifle and full gear for two hours. At some point Martti got fed up with it and punched the NCO, which meant more difficulties for Martti. Most of the Finnish men adjusted slowly to the German discipline, but things started to work, especially when the combat training began.

SS-Schütze Martti Lehtonen (in the center) with his comrades in Graz, Austria.

The facilities in Schönbrunn were good enough for the basic training but they weren't good for shooting and realistic combat training. For this the combat training, the battalion was transferred back to Stralsund. The battalion stayed and trained in Stralsund from July 9 to August 25 (1941). The terrain in Stralsund was much more suitable for combat training and there were proper shooting ranges. As mentioned before, the Finnish men weren't exactly enthusiastic about the German drill exercises, but at the shooting range they got excellent results. Those results were so good that it had a positive effect on the relationship between Finnish volunteers and German NCOs. Of course the best shooters got rewards such as extra leave. On August 3 the battalion got new rifles which were the ones for combat use and these new rifles proved to be very effective in the hands of Finnish soldiers. The average score at the shooting range for a German Battalion was 23.0 points. The Finnish Battalion shot an average of 28.2 points! At the same time the men were given their combat assignments (who was going to operate as machine gun crew, sharpshooter, etc.). In Stralsund the battalion also received its trucks as the Wiking Division was a motorized unit. A selection of men was sent to driving courses to operate these trucks.

There were some quite significant circumstances that made the men complain: the lack of food during the long training days, the lack of washing facilities and healthcare, etc. Another problem was that the battalion had too many German NCOs and officers in the Finnish ranks and there weren't any vacancies for Finns in these ranks. The Finnish Foreign Ministry had sent Lieutenant Colonel K.E. Levälahti to Germany for supervising duties, and he managed to get some improvements through to make the situation more tolerable for the men.

The final phases of the combat training were carried out in the large training center of Gross-Born (Truppenübungsplatz Gross-Born) in Pomerania. It was located at about 300 km east of Stralsund. The battalion was transferred to Gross-Born by train on August 25, 1941. This training center was so large that only one panzer division could operate in the training area! The Finns were informed that the area itself was 30 km in length and 15 km wide. There were also 6 movie theaters and 24 canteens. The Finnish Battalion stayed in Gross-Born for two and a half months. The training was divided into four phases: the first phase (began on August 25) contained basic infantry combat skills; the second phase was squad and platoon

Rottenführer Martti Lehtonen – FFB/4.kp – Finnisches Freiwilligen Bataillon der Waffen SS/4. Kp.

combat training that lasted from September 1 to September 21; during the third phase training was extended to company formations (September 22 to October 2); the fourth and final phase was an exercise for the whole battalion (October 3-5).

It was a rainy Sunday on October 15, 1941 when the Finnish Battalion had their swearing-in ceremony in Gross-Born. The Germans had planned that this ceremony would be grand, and the event had to symbolize the German-Finnish comradeship. The Finnish Foreign Ministry didn't share these thoughts with the Germans though. The Finnish Ambassador in Berlin had orders from the Finnish Foreign Ministry not to take part in the ceremony. Because of the Finnish reluctant attitude, the Germans were not able to send any high level officials to the ceremony. The Finnish military attaché, Colonel Walter Horn, presented the flag of the battalion. The flag was designed and made in Finland. A parade was held after the ceremony, and there was a big feast for the battalion and their guests which lasted until the early morning hours.

The men assumed that the battalion would get its orders and begin their deployment to the Eastern Front straight after the swearing-in ceremonies. But the news came that they wouldn't be deployed for at least another two weeks. At the end of October the battalion packed their gear, prepared the trucks, and got ready for their deployment to the front. However just before the set date their orders were cancelled and the battalion had to stand down. The men's excitement changed suddenly into a great disappointment. It took almost two months until new marching orders were given, and the battalion began its journey to the front. During that two month period, the men became frustrated and there where at least two times when the battalion packed and got ready, but then the orders were cancelled at the last moment. Of course the battalion commander tried to keep the morale up, and during that time the battalion had additional exercises. Frustration of constant waiting sometimes boiled over, and disciplinary actions had to be taken. This stand still situation was also suitable for spreading all kinds of rumors. There were rumors that the battalion would be changed into a ski-equipped troop and sent to the Alps for training, or that the battalion would be heading to France or back to Finland. Finally on the night of November 30, a phone call from SS-Führungshauptamt was made to battalion commander Collani. The orders were that the battalion would be immediately transported to Berdichev by train. Preparations began at once, and on December 3 the first elements of the battalion boarded the train and left Gross-Born.

The Long March to the Front

On December 2, Martti and the other men of the 4th Company loaded their trucks and drove to the train station. The whole 4th Company needed two long trains for their vehicles and other equipment. Transports started the very next morning. During December 3-4, one company at a time left Gross-Born: one in the morning and one in the evening. The trains passed Graudenz and from there to Modlin and to Warsaw. From Warsaw the trains continued to Lublin – Chelm – Lubomilin – Kovel. The trains passed Berdichev on December 7, and the entire battalion arrived at Vinnytsia (Vinnitsa) on December 8. Vinnytsia, a city in west-central Ukraine, was also the location of Hitler's headquarters for the eastern front operations. This headquarter was better known as Führerhauptquartier Werwolf. At Vinnytsia men also heard the news that England had declared war on Finland and that Japan had attacked Pearl Harbor. The battalion was ordered to continue to Stalino (current: Donetsk) by trucks. That meant approximately 835 km, and it was estimated to take 10 days to complete the trip.

Rottenführer Martti Lehtonen – FFB/4.kp – Finnisches Freiwilligen Bataillon der Waffen SS/4. Kp.

Every company was ready on the morning of December 10 and their motorized march began. The first objective was Gaisin (Gaysinskiy district) which was 95 km from Vinnytsia. There were no major difficulties on the road, and the battalion arrived in Gaisin in the afternoon. Roads were muddy and icy, but the battalion still managed to get to its destination with only some minor damage on trucks and sidecars. After spending the night in some old Russian barracks, the battalion left Gaisin in the early hours of December 11.

As it has been repeated many times before on the eastern front the Germans had two enemies: Russians and Mother Nature itself. The winter in the Ukrainian steppe also slowly became a harsh reality for the Finns. From Gaisin to Uman, the road conditions worsened, and the signs of battles were seen everywhere as there were destroyed tanks and vehicles along the road. The mud was getting thicker and trucks were getting stuck in it and oncoming units started to cause traffic jams. Battalion commander Collani decided that the battalion would take a rest at Uman. The battalion managed get to Uman, and the next day the weather conditions worsened. The battalion traveled almost 90 km to a village called Dobrovlitskov. Martti's 4th Company managed to find a good place to stay overnight in two old schools in the village.

The 4th Company had to leave five light trucks behind when the march continued the next morning. Other companies also had similar vehicle problems. The repair units hadn't reached the battalion yet, so there was nothing that could be done with the vehicles that had broken down due to the weather conditions. At this point there were practically no roads left as they were all transformed into mud, but that didn't stop them at all and a huge effort was made and the battalion moved 50 km forward to Rovnoje. These severe weather conditions also meant that fuel consumption was increasing rapidly. There wasn't enough fuel for every truck, and the 2nd Company had to stay in Rovnoje when the rest of the battalion left on December 14 to continue to its next destination of Kropyvnytskyi (Kirovograd).

There was no change in the weather, and the roads weren't getting any better. Mud, mud, and only mud! A lot of trucks got stuck on the side of the "road", but somehow the battalion's three companies managed to reach Kropyvnytskyi without the loss of any trucks. It took five hours to travel that 50 km! The battalion was ordered to fuel up in Kropyvnytskyi, but once they arrived the fuel wasn't there. The battalion commander had some huge problems getting the fuel supply up there, and the battalion had to halt its march for six days. These six days at Kropyvnytskyi actually gave the mechanics a chance to make truck repairs, and gave the men some much needed rest. The 2nd Company which was left behind also had to get their fuel supplied and were able to get some rest. In Kropyvnytskyi it was clear that the war started to come closer as during the night there was the constant firing which could be heard from a distance. Unfortunately, six Germans were killed just before the battalion arrived in Kropyvnytskyi. A reconnaissance patrol was sent out on December 19 to see what the conditions were like in the immediate area of the village. Obviously they weren't good at all, but on December 20 the temperature dropped and all the roads turned into ice. The 1st and 3rd Company got their orders to move out and drove 75 km to Oleksandriia. Martti's 4th Company and the 2nd Company drove that same route the next day. The weather was good so the next objective was to get 90 km forward to Alferovo. Not all the units made it to Alferovo as the freezing temperatures started to cause troubles when the wheels of parked trucks froze solid into mud. Due to the lack of glycol, it meant that the radiator of every vehicle had to be emptied, and the lack of water supplies caused delays in the troops' advance. From Alferovo the battalion headed to Dnepropetrovsk.

Rottenführer Martti Lehtonen – FFB/4.kp – Finnisches Freiwilligen Bataillon der Waffen SS/4. Kp.

Dnepropetrovsk was and still is one of the Ukraine's largest cities and on December 22 the main body of the battalion arrived there. Road conditions improved, and the last kilometers were paved road. The 4th Company arrived in Dnepropetrovsk on December 23. There wasn't any room for the battalion to settle because the whole city was crowded by German troops. After a while, a former museum of the Russian revolution was made available for the battalion's use. It was Christmastime and the men had some free time to see the city. On Christmas Eve the battalion gathered for dinner and Christmas trees were decorated in their quarters. The Christmas dinner itself was plentiful: among many other things, a whole grilled chicken was served to every man! Men had bought vodka in Kropyvnytskyi and after those bottles were opened, the atmosphere started to get quite chaotic. During the evening some group of Finns pushed a large statue of Stalin down some stairs. The statue was made out of plaster, and it broke in a thousand pieces. The battalion stayed four days in Dnepropetrovsk and then continued their march towards Stalino (Donetsk) on December 28. At this point the battalion had been on route for 26 days. When the orders were given in the beginning of December, the estimated duration was 10 days. This gives some kind of perspective about the obstacles and distances the battalion had to face to get to the front.

The 2nd Company had received orders from the staff of the 1. Panzer Army (1. Panzerarmee) that the company had to get to Stalino as soon as possible. The 2nd Company was put on a train and left Dnepropetrovsk on December 29. The rest of the battalion continued their advance by trucks the same day. Everything went smoothly for the first day as the conditions were better because the snow paved the roads. The 1st Company drove almost 145 km, 3rd Company 100 km, and 4th Company traveled 115 km on that day. The endless and terrible muddy and swampy roads had slowed down the battalion's advance from the beginning but now the struggle against winter had started. The next morning on December 30 the temperature had dropped so low that there were great difficulties to get the trucks' engines running. It had also snowed so much that because of the high snow banks it was extremely difficult to start towing the trucks. But somehow they were able to get the trucks on the road again and continued their advance. The wind was blowing very hard on the Ukrainian steppe and combined with the continuous snow, it made visibility zero. Because of the strong winds, big snow banks had formed all over the terrain. During the day, the troops' advance was somehow still possible but at night, in complete darkness, there wasn't any chance to move forward. Trucks and other vehicles were getting stuck in snow and needed towing, and some trucks were left on the road overnight. During the next three days problems started to pile up even more. Snow storms continued and blocked all the roads. There weren't enough snow plows to clean the roads and many trucks had broken down. The amount of driveable trucks dwindled, and at a certain point there wasn't enough transport capacity for the troops. At this point it became clear that there weren't any other possibilities to continue forward by truck, so the main elements of the battalion had been stuck in a town called Mezevaya. From there battalion commander, Collani managed to organize a train transport to Stalino. The 1st Company left Mezevaya by train on January 4. The 3rd Company was loaded on a train at Grisino three days later.

Martti's 4th Company had been stuck for a couple days at Slavjanka because the roads were busy with oncoming traffic. Slavjanka was a village near Mezevaya. After roads were cleared of traffic, the entire 4th Company was gathered at Mezevaya. There the company found empty barns which were used as a shelter for the trucks. Empty oil barrels were used for fires to warm up the barns.

Rottenführer Martti Lehtonen – FFB/4.kp – Finnisches Freiwilligen Bataillon der Waffen SS/4. Kp.

The barns were big enough to shelter two trucks. Two trucks at a time were towed inside a warm barn were engines were able to start after warm-up and checked for possible damages or failures. The weather cleared, and during the early hours the company headed to Stalino. From there they moved to Rutshenkovo which was the battalion's ordered destination.

On January 8, the first units of the battalion arrived at Rutshenkovo which was just behind the Mius River front. In Rutshenkovo there was a reinforcement center for the troops. The main elements of the battalion arrived at this destination, and after a journey that took almost a month, the battalion commander sent a notification to the SS-Führungshauptamt that the marching orders were fulfilled. Commander Collani was promoted to SS-Sturmbannführer a couple of days prior to his arrival in Rutshenkovo. It seemed like a reward for him for having completed the training and executing the marching orders in a timely manner. Although the whole battalion hadn't yet reached Rutshenkovo, there were still some units that were on their way. It actually took almost to the end of January when everyone finally arrived. These kinds of desperate marches were common during the winter of 1941-1942 on the Eastern Front, and some may question how reasonable and useful these kind of forced movements were. Of the battalion's 221 vehicles, only 114 managed to get to Rutshenkovo. From the 114 vehicles, only 80 were still running and drivable! The rest of the trucks and cars needed repairs and some needed to be replaced. The cost of just getting one battalion to the front seemed terribly high.

In Rutshenkovo the battalion was attached to the Wiking Division and it was given a new name: IV/Nordland (IV Battalion of the Nordland Regiment). The decision of discharging the excess of Finnish officers and NCOs was made and about 140 men were sent back to Germany, and from there back to Finland. So called "division men" who had fought in the Wiking Division since the beginning of the war, were ordered to join the battalion. It meant that 100 men were added to the battalion's strength. The Finns were now all in the same unit. On January 12, the commander of the Wiking Division, SS-Gruppenführer Felix Steiner, ordered the battalion to stay in the city of Amvrosiivka as a motorized reserve for the division. The battalion moved to Amvrosiivka on January 18.

Spilling Blood on Foreign Soil: the Mius River Front Line

Division commander Steiner inspected the Finnish Battalion at Amvrosiivka on January 18, 1942. The next day the battalion was gathered in the local theater were commander Steiner gave a speech to the new men of the Wiking Division. Those Finnish volunteers who were there always remembered how commander Steiner shook hands with every soldier and talked personally to the men. This gesture formed trust and confidence in their commander among the Finns, and was one of the things that created the bond between men and their commander, and it lasted to the very end. Steiner visited Finland after the war in 1956 and met his former brothers-in-arms. Some Finnish volunteers also traveled to Germany to meet their commander.

Commander Steiner had a meeting with battalion commander Collani and the company commanders on January 20. It was decided that the Finnish Battalion would relieve one Slovakian Battalion on the front line and take their positions. At that time, the war was in a stage where neither side was active and it had become a trench war. Front lines had been stabilized for the winter months, and the Germans thought that it was a good time to put the battalion in action. Preparations started right away, and the Finnish Battalion was moved to the front line during the night of January 21-22.

Rottenführer Martti Lehtonen – FFB/4.kp – Finnisches Freiwilligen Bataillon der Waffen SS/4. Kp.

The battalion's sector length was 2-2.5 km. Bunkers and trenches were placed on the high ridge that followed the river Mius. The length of the front line was a normal sector for a German Battalion on the front. When the Finnish Battalion took these positions at the front, their number was a bit larger than the standard German Battalion. The order of battle was as follows: the 3rd Company on the right side; 1st Company on the left; 2nd Company was the reserve; the 4th Company, which was the battalion's heavy artillery company, was spread around the front line. The normal rotation for companies was 20 days at the front followed by 10 in reserve. When the Finns got settled in they noticed right away how poorly the Slovakians had made their fortifications. Trenches weren't deep enough, and bunkers had been constructed very lightly. The work for improvements began right away. It was possible to do some repair work because it was a very calm time at the front lines. Everything was done by the field manual: all the shooting sectors were carefully chosen for every weapon, and all the proper documents about the bases were composed with great accuracy.

The newly-trained Finnish soldiers were eager and energetic when they finally had a chance to show their skills. It didn't take long when the long days in trenches got to them. Even though the Finns almost rebuilt everything, the living conditions in the trenches were still sometimes intolerable. Temperature dropped sometimes to -30 degrees Celsius and with strong winds it felt even colder. Trenches were filled with snow all the time, and frostbite sent many men to field hospitals. The dirty uniforms and lice were a constant headache too, but there was one bigger problem that they had to deal with: hunger. Hunger was omnipresent as the food was mainly millet porridge and dry food. It wasn't very nutritious which resulted in many of the men's health became weaker and weaker. It was at that time that Martti and one other man came from a sauna which was good for getting rid of the lice. After the sauna, they were supposed to get a meal, but when Martti and his comrade came to the kitchen, the cook had already served all the food and there was nothing left. First there was some shouting but soon the fists started flying. The cook got beaten up and the men decided to take all the food they could find and bring it to the others at the front. It didn't take long before they were caught and taken to rear to hear and face their punishment. This time justice was merciful and everything was settled. It was clear that the men reacted this way because of hunger.

Although the overall situation was fairly quiet at the front it was still a warzone. Snipers were active all the time and artillery/mortar barrages caused a lot of casualties and damage. Both sides were active in patrolling and tried to capture prisoners. Minefields also took their toll when some unfortunate patrols walked into them. As mid-March approached, the battalion had lost 12 men (KIA) and 33 had been wounded. When adding the men who were in field hospitals for other reasons, the number goes up to almost 100! The warming weather of the spring didn't help the situation because then some other diseases, such as hepatitis A and influenza, started to spread. Finally on April 24, the order came to switch to new positions close to the village of Oleksandrivka (Aleksandrovka).

Martti wrote in his diary that he arrived in Oleksandrivka on April 25, 1942. He described the trenches and bunkers as in better shape compared to the ones they occupied back in January. Martti's squad almost got hit by friendly fire - which happened every now and then at the front - when their own artillery almost hit their bunker. Otherwise there weren't any other incidents when the battalion settled to their new positions. The time in Oleksandrivka turned out to be peaceful, and it was a quiet time at the front. The warm spring days made life in the trenches much more bearable. The days went on as usual on the front lines: patrolling, guard duty, and digging new

Rottenführer Martti Lehtonen – FFB/4.kp – Finnisches Freiwilligen Bataillon der Waffen SS/4. Kp.

trenches and bunkers. The Finns proved themselves to the Germans that they were extremely skilled in building duties. Commander Collani and other officers noticed this and gave his men credit. This was mentioned in the official reports which was greatly appreciated by the troops. A good example of such recognition was that commander Collani gave a bottle of vodka and chocolate to the men who had built a bunker exceptionally well. Martti also wrote in his diary that on May 2 he and four other men got a bottle of wine.

The German forces were now preparing for the upcoming summer offensive. The Wiking Division was also reorganized, and the Finnish Battalion was renamed on May 25, 1942: III (Finn.)/SS-Regiment Nordland. The battalion's companies' orders were also changed: the 1st Company became the 9th Company; the 2nd became the 10th; the 3rd the 11th; and Martti's 4th Company became the 12th. The Finns weren't quite pleased with the new name. They had used the unofficial name "Finnische Jägerbataillon" so far, but there was already a unit named after Jägers in the Wehrmacht so they had to relinquish the name. Summer came, and on the front lines the battle operations diminished to a minimum in the battalion's sector. The Russians weren't active either. In Martti's diary, the days in May and June were almost identical. The days mainly consisted of patrolling and building and fortifying positions. The men swam in the river and bathed in the sun during their free time. Sometimes they managed to get some wine or other alcoholic drinks. Martti mentioned that on a couple occasions he got way too drunk and lost all his money on a card game. Of course training was still carried out, but not in large scale. Because there wasn't much fighting during those days, the minefields became the worst enemies of the soldiers, and the landmines caused a lot of casualties. In the morning of June 19, Martti's squad left on a patrol. During that patrol in the town of Demikovka, he stepped on mine and sustained injuries on his right hand. He was carried to the rear and transported further to Uspenskaja. From there Martti was evacuated by train to the SS-Lazarett in Dnepropetrowsk. Martti spent only a week and a half there, suggesting that his wounds weren't that bad, as his recovery time was pretty short. Luck was certainly on his side the day he stepped on that landmine!

Finnish volunteers during training in the village of Demidovka (Ukraine) - summer 1942. From left to right: unknown, Yrjö Rouhiainen, Olof Jakobsson, Matti Niemi, Mauno Rytilahti, Sakari Sarpola, Hugo Berglund and Martti Lehtonen.

The Finnish Battalion was pulled from the front line on July 9, and was ordered to march to the village of Mokry Jelantsky (Mokri Jelantsik). There the goal was to get the battalion combat ready for the upcoming offensive. For this particular reason, they were sent to rear for another training phase. The battalion also received new weapons at this time, and the men needed training to get acquainted with them. Martti was still at the hospital during this period. Training

Rottenführer Martti Lehtonen – FFB/4.kp – Finnisches Freiwilligen Bataillon der Waffen SS/4. Kp.

started in Mokry Jelantsky on July 14 and lasted until August 8. Martti arrived in Mokry Jelantsky on July 16, although he hadn't completely recovered and was unable to carry anything heavy. Martti's health improved after a couple days, and he participated in the complete training. As it reads in Martti's diary, the days in Mokry Jelantsky were like the days in basic training: the days started early (0300-0400) and lasted to late in the evening. In his diary was an entry that on August 1 they were training and shooting with their new 5 cm PAK 38 anti-tank guns. One round fell short and it wounded the commander of the 12th Company, named Bruckner, in the chest. The Finnish Battalion was armed with 3.7 cm PAK 36 anti-tank guns when they went to the front. During the time in Mokry Jelantsky the battalion's heavy weaponry was significantly reinforced. At the beginning of August the battalion's heavy weaponry consisted of 61 light machine guns, 12 heavy machine guns, three light mortars (5 cm Leichte Granatwerfer 36), and 12 medium mortars (8 cm GrW 34), four heavy anti-tank guns (5 cm PAK), and four cannons. At the same time, the 5. SS-Panzer-Abteilung (main armor of this unit were then Panzer III and Panzer IV) was attached to the Wiking Division. This Panzer-Abteilung was commanded by SS-Sturmbannführer Johannes Mühlenkamp. Mühlenkamp rose to the ranks of division commander later in the war, and was the recipient of the Knight's Cross of the Iron Cross with Oak Leaves.

Fall Blau was launched on June 28, 1942. It was Hitler's major offensive to seize the rich oil fields of the Caucasus. The Germans' oil supplies got a major blow with the defeats suffered in the African theatre. At the beginning of 1942, Hitler had already stated that the next objective of this war would be oil, and that the oil fields of South Caucasus were the solution to this problem. All reorganizations, reinforcements, and arrangements that had been undertaken during the spring and summer time - also within the

Finnish Battalion - were all executed to prepare for this main offensive in the Caucasus. The plan for Army Group South was to advance east towards Stalingrad and then encircle the Russian troops between the rivers Don and Volga. The German forces would the sweep to the south towards the Caucasus and seize the oil fields.

The Spearhead of the Caucasus Offensive – from the Don to Maykop

The Finnish Battalion's participation in the battle of Caucasus, Fall Blau, was the hardest and bloodiest part in their war. The 5. SS-Panzer-Division Wiking and its Finnish soldiers formed, several times, the spearhead of the attacks. While the Finnish Battalion was still in Mokry Jelantsky getting to know their new weapons and getting trained, the rest of the Wiking Division units were fighting and pushing towards their objectives. The Wiking Division had taken part in the battle of Rostov in July, and was heading to the Maykop oil fields in the southern Caucasus as a spearhead division of the 1st Panzer Army. The division distinguished itself in these battles so well that it was mentioned four times in the Wehrmachtbericht. All of Army Group South's armies had been gaining great victories right from the beginning of the operation. The offensive slammed through the Russian lines, and the Red Army was under heavy attack. These victories gave Hitler a false image of the capabilities and force of Army Group South, and he decided to divide Army Group South into two army groups: Army Group A would head south to seize the oil fields, and Army Group B would keep going towards Stalingrad. Rather than first reaching the river Volga and then turn south, his forces would now do this simultaneously. Hitler's generals warned him about the risks and how this would weaken the force of the attack. As we now know, the mistake that Hitler made with this decision turned the tide of the Eastern Front.

Rottenführer Martti Lehtonen – FFB/4.kp – Finnisches Freiwilligen Bataillon der Waffen SS/4. Kp.

The scorching heat and flying dust were new conditions the Finnish men had to deal with. The battalion left Mokry Jelantsky on August 10 at sunrise. Martti's company drove almost 220 km in one day. They stayed overnight in tents, and continued their advance the next morning. The Finnish Battalion was on its way to catch up with the rest of the Wiking Division's units. The next stretch for Martti's company was also over 220 km. The men were exhausted because of the hot weather, and the dust was flying everywhere. There were large numbers of other units driving fast through the Russian steppes, and it was truly an atmosphere of a blitzkrieg. Tanks, trucks, airplanes, and columns of men, all going in the same direction. The Finnish Battalion traveled more than 700 km in only three days! German Engineer Battalions had repaired the blown up bridges along the way, and roads were back in good shape. This was a completely different experience than the one the battalion had when it first arrived at the front lines.

The battalion arrived at its destination on August 13: a place called Komsomolakya. There at the division's headquarters, the battalion was put on guard duty. The Wiking Division was the spearhead of Army Group A and the front lines were close. There wasn't much rest after the march, and the battalion received the orders to advance. The village of Lineinaya was fortified by a Russian cavalry unit. The battalion's orders were to take the village and its surroundings at all costs. The population of Lineinaya was maybe just over 2000 people, and all the houses in the village were made out of clay. It was mainly a Russian collective farm (kolkhoz) located on a hillside. The Russian cavalry had fortified their positions on the surrounding hills, and the village itself was their stronghold. On August 16, 1942 at 0330h, the Finnish Battalion started moving towards the village. There were 52 tanks taking part in this attack. Most of the men were sitting on top of the tanks when they moved forward. As soon as the Russians opened fire, the men jumped off the tanks to take cover. At first the Russian were quite intense in their offensive but as the German tanks move forward the Russians started to pull back. Martti wrote in his diary that after "two hours of fighting" they were able to seize the village. Some officers (such as the battalion SS-Hauptsturmführer Erwin H. Reichel) of the Westland Regiment's staff were observing this attack. Reichel commended the Finnish Battalion, and said that it looked as if the Germans had been the ones doing the fighting. The battalion lost four men in total (incl. two officers), and seven were wounded. The Finnish Battalion afterwards gathered their war booty: two cannons, two anti-tank cannons, five mortars, handguns, horses, and maybe most important of all, they took 34 Russian prisoners. This was the first major operation for the Finnish Battalion and also their first experience with the German "blitzkrieg" tactics. The battalion showed that it was up to the task!

After seizing the village, the battalion stayed there for over a week. The Westland Regiment continued to chase the retreating Russian units. The people of the village were friendly towards the occupiers during the day, but at night their attitude changed significantly. During the day there weren't any confrontations and usually men traded soap and gasoline with the villagers for bread and eggs. Everything seemed to be alright, but after sunset things got hostile. One night someone tried to burn the battalion's trucks and the Finns got shot at. Martti wrote in his diary that for him the days he spent in Lineiyana he was only on guard duty but nothing more. Possibly Martti's squad didn't have any problems with the locals. He doesn't mention anything about confrontations with the locals.

By the end August of 1942, the Russian Army's resistance grew and their defenses started to hold as German forces were closing in towards the mountain passes. Hitler's objective in this sector was to

Rottenführer Martti Lehtonen – FFB/4.kp – Finnisches Freiwilligen Bataillon der Waffen SS/4. Kp.

get to the shores of Black Sea. The city of Tuapse was one of targets. Division commander Steiner was very skeptical about the change of plan to get through the mountain passes and break the Russian defense lines. The Westland Regiment functioned as the spearhead, once again, but they hadn't enough force to push through. The Wiking Division had already suffered significant losses which brought the manpower down to a low number. Also, the effects of Hitler's decision of dividing the army group's forces started to show as the Russians were slowly gaining control of the situation.

The Finnish Battalion marched from Lineinaya to Kabardinskaya on August 25-26. However the assault was halted, and the battalion had to dig itself in and a new trench war started again. Their stay in Kabardinskaya lasted almost three weeks. During that time there were only a few small skirmishes between patrols, but nothing major happened. The Russian Air Force was also very active and bombed the German positions without mercy. Russian artillery barrages also caused many casualties. Now the fall was knocking on the door, which meant dropping temperatures at night time and lots of rain. After a while, the men were getting sick again with flu and other diseases. Martti wrote in his diary that their squad had only a few peaceful days during their time in Kabardinskaya. There were small patrol fights or the Russians bombed the place. He also mentioned several Russian defectors, and that on August 28-29, a total of eight Russians approached Martti's squad's positions and surrendered themselves. They took the prisoners and escorted them to company headquarters for interrogation. These Russian soldiers had automatic rifles which Martti and his comrade took for their own use. During the interrogations the prisoners told the Germans that 10 km to west of Kabardinskaya the 32nd Division of the Russian Army was posted. It had arrived on the front lines five days before. Upon hearing this, regiment commander von Scholz immediately made new arrangements for the regiment's defensive positions.

Even though the German offensive was slowing down, they still had managed to gain one of their objectives: the Maykop oilfields. The Finnish Battalion's stay in Kabardinskaya was part of the task to secure these oil fields. Martti wrote an entry in his diary that when his unit moved to their new positions on September 1, he had seen many oil wells but all of them had been deliberately damaged. Retreating Russians had destroyed all of the oil fields and oil refineries. The destruction was done so thoroughly that the Germans estimated that it would take them at least one year to get the wells operational again. The fuel supply of the German forces where still depending on Romanian oil, and the long supply route caused stoppages on the German advance. So even this small German victory didn't make any changes to the overall situation.

The Battles of the Terek River

At the same time the Wiking Division was advancing towards the Caucasus Mountains, there were other Army Group A units that were fighting their way towards the oil fields of Baku. By the end of August, the German forces had reached the Terek River in the Eastern Caucasus. The Wehrmacht's 3rd Panzer Division seized Mozdok on August 24-25 while suffering heavy casualties. This became the German bridgehead in Terek. The town of Mozdok was the farthest point in Russia that Germans reached during the war. The plan was to continue the assault from Mozdok to Grozny, the capital of Chechnya, and at the same time to cut off the old Georgian military road which functioned as a supply line and retreat route for the Russians. The oil fields of Grozny were almost within their reach - only 100 km from the Mozdok bridgehead. But the Germans were struggling, and they suffered many casualties and fuel shortages. In

Rottenführer Martti Lehtonen – FFB/4.kp – Finnisches Freiwilligen Bataillon der Waffen SS/4. Kp.

the meantime, the Russians were sending reinforcements to the front lines and began to push the Germans back. To keep the offensive progress going the German commanders sent units from the Western Caucasus to the Terek front. The Wiking Division was also one those units which was ordered to move to Terek. Martti already heard rumors a few days before the orders came in that the battalion would leave Kabardinskaya for the Terek front. On September 16, the battalion started preparations for the upcoming move to the Terek front. The next day the battalion was on the road and they drove their trucks and panzers almost 600 km to the east towards the banks of the Terek River in the area of Malgobek. This journey took them five days before they reached their destination. Malgobek was a town 50 km south of Mozdok. At its destination the battalion was attached to the LII Army Corps commanded by General Eugen Ott. The exhausted German forces in this sector were in desperate need of reinforcements, and the Wiking Division was immediately thrown into battle when it arrived. On September 21, the battalion reported that their fighting strength consisted of 29 officers, 178 NCOs, and 509 soldiers. The troops headed to Mozdok the following day, but they were called back. Martti wrote that they didn't know the reason why the orders were cancelled, but the next day around noon they moved across the Terek River and took up their positions near Malgobek. The Finnish Battalion was ordered to take the 666th Infantry Regiment's positions. This particular regiment had been in bloody battles before, and it was completely beaten up when the Finns came and replaced them on the front. The Finnish Battalion had more men at their disposal than the 666th which gives some perspective of the losses suffered on the Terek Front and how fierce the fighting had been in that area. The Finnish men knew right away that they were thrown into the meat grinder, and the consequences would become visible after a couple of days at the front.

Germania's Assault Generation

Malgobek lies in mountainous terrain: high hills, no trees, and only knee-high grass provided some form of cover for the infantry soldiers. One of those many hills received a new name from the Finnish soldiers: the "Kill-Hill". The date for a new attack was set, and the commander of the 1st Panzer Army, von Kleist, ordered the Wiking Division to form the spearhead. The attack was set to begin on September 26, and the objective was a village called Sagopshin, located approximately 20 km to the east from their current location. Sagopshin was just beside the Georgian military road, and the railroad to Grozny ran straight through the village. To take control of these routes would mean serious trouble for the Russian 9th Army troops.

On Thursday, September 24, Martti wrote: *"We took new positions on the hills. We were shooting. I'm feeling ill and I'm in terrible condition. Ate some dry food. Also ate some raw meat in the evening."* The next day Martti had a terrible case of diarrhea, and his condition got even worse. He didn't eat anything the whole day. Even in his condition, Martti and the whole battalion prepared for the next day's attack. The H-hour was set: Saturday, September 26 at 0500h.

Initially only the 11th Company of the Finnish Battalion was sent to battle. Martti's unit was attached to the 11th Company, so he was there right from the beginning. The 11th Company managed to conquer the first hill after 30 minutes of fighting. The Russians didn't give an inch back, and they just fell where they stood. However that first half hour of combat caused several casualties for the 11th Company: four dead and eight wounded. During the next four hours of fighting, the company lost another 10 men (KIA) and 30 were wounded. In the afternoon, the company continued towards the next ridge which was their next objective. This time the Russians proved too tough to beat, and the 11th Company had to halt their attack. At

Rottenführer Martti Lehtonen – FFB/4.kp – Finnisches Freiwilligen Bataillon der Waffen SS/4. Kp.

sunrise they pulled back to the hill which they took earlier that morning. The company had lost 25 men (KIA) and 54 were wounded. Among the Finnish volunteers, these events would later be known as the battles of Kill-Hill. Later, as the veterans wrote memoirs or told about this battle, many told that the training which they received in Gross-Born prepared them well for these hard fought battles. As they were advancing on open terrain against fortified positions under heavy fire they tried to do like they were taught: crawl, heels down, shoulders down, fast stride, and back down again. Of course nothing can prepare you for seeing your comrade blown to pieces or take a bullet to the head, but for surviving in those harsh conditions their training seemed to be very useful.

The next day the 11th Company stayed in reserve. The men dug foxholes and stayed in them as it was the 9th and 10th Companies' turn to attack. The Russian Air Force had gained air superiority over this part of the front lines, and several air assaults were made to support their ground troops. The Russian Army had also brought Katyusha rocket launchers to the front, and this rocket barrage was something which the Finns hadn't faced before. By the end of September 28, the 9th and 10th Companies had gained control of three hills and had advanced almost 6 km. The companies started to dig themselves in and took defensive positions on the conquered hills. On the third day of the battle, the battalion didn't manage to advance at all. The 11th Company was ordered to the front, and the whole battalion was together again. The men were exhausted because the days were hot and they didn't have any water left. The water and food supply didn't work at all and they had to stay in their foxholes for long periods of time without food or water. After three days of constant fighting, the Wiking Division was at the outskirts of Sagopshin, but Malgobek was still in the hands of the Russian forces.

Germania's Assault Generation

In the big picture, this progress wasn't enough for Army Group commanders. The Wiking Division's commander Steiner and LII Army Group commander, General Ott, had different opinions how to continue the assault and how the Wiking Division's units should be used at the front. This quarrel got so tense that the matter got all the way up to Himmler, and the 1st Panzer Army's commander von Kleist. This caused reproaches from von Kleist, and a notice was sent to the high command of Waffen SS in Berlin.

"Thursday October 1, 42: We got moving at night. Our aim was to take the village. Every company in our battalion was taking part in this (1st Platoon, 1 mortar, 1 MG) but we still didn't succeed. Ruskies held their ground! We have been fighting the entire day and we're surrounded. Now the Ruskies are attacking our right flank, time is 1530h."

Between October 1-6, the German forces (Wehrmacht 111th Division, 370th Division, 13th Panzer Division, and the 5. SS-Panzer Division Wiking) tried to find a weak spot in the Russian lines to break through. The assault advanced so that the 111th Division, reinforced with Wiking's Germania Regiment, took the town of Malgobek and its surrounding hills on October 6. The Finnish Battalion was with the Nordland Regiment but the sector they were in wasn't the focal point at the time. In the Nordland Regiment's sector the attacks had petered out. The attack on October 1 was their last one in their sector, then the battalion was transported to their new position on October 7

The battalion took up new positions just south of Malgobek on October 7, and right away they were charging the hills once again. All companies started to advance just after noon. Both sides' artillery were firing heavy barrages. Right after the start, the battalion was pinned down in a crossfire. They took fire from three directions: from the front, from their right, and from the southern flank. Slowly but steadily, the battalion managed to conquer yet another hill and received the orders to dig in to fortify their position. The next morning the men were on the move again. This time 11th Company rushed forward and managed to take the ridge ahead of them. Other companies tried to follow but they had to cross a cornfield which was full of hiding Russians. Four Russian tanks also made a counter-attack to the flank. By nightfall, the 9th and 10th Companies had cleared the entire cornfield, and had pushed through to the same point as the 11th Company. The price of these victories was 3 killed and 24 wounded. One of the wounded was 10th Company's commander Porsch. But there was no time to breathe as the battalion was again switching positions. This time the battalion was ordered to move north to Hill 698 (meaning the height of the hill) which was little over 2 km north of a point called Malgobek II. When the battalion arrived at its new destination, the 10th and 11th Companies had to be merged into one company. Both companies had suffered such severe losses that it was reasonable to join the remaining men into a new unit.

The Finnish Battalion was detached from the Nordland Regiment and attached to the Germania Regiment which at that time was under the command of the 111th Infantry Division. So General Steiner wasn't in charge, and the battalion would get its order from General Hermann Recknagel who was the commander of 111th Infantry Division. The first orders were to take Hill 701.

SS-Obersturmführer Tauno Pohjanlehto gathered a patrol for a reconnaissance mission to Hill 701. Pohjanlehto reported to battalion commander Collani after they returned from their patrol. The terrain on Hill 701 was suitable for the defender: there was a downward slope of about 300 meters in length where the attackers would be under fire from three directions; front and both flanks. Pohjanlehto's patrol lost four men who sustained injuries during the reconnaissance. It was a suicide mission to attack that hill, and

Germania's Assault Generation

Collani contacted Germania Regiment's staff and tried to change the plan, but they refused. There was nothing he could do and the attack was set to begin on Friday, October 9 around noon.

The German artillery fired smoke shells on the hill, and the 11th Company started moving under a smoke screen. It didn't take long before things turned the way as they had expected: the Russians opened fire from all three directions and their artillery and mortars joined the "festivities" while shooting heavy and accurate barrages. The Russians also had tanks in their defensive lines which had a straight line of fire towards the attacker. There was no possibility whatsoever to advance on Hill 701. Men had to dig in and find cover. The Germania Regiment's commander had to accept the fact that the defender had the upper hand, and he was forced to order the battalion to take defensive positions. It was planned that the battalion would continue their attack the next morning, but the Russians were determined and launched a counter-attack against the Germania Regiment's lines.

"Saturday October 10 – 42: This day was hard. The Ruskies had been hitting us constantly with heavy force. We've been running back and forth the lines. Now their tanks are coming. The time is 1700h."

In the morning of October 10, the Russian artillery started pounding the German positions. The artillery and mortar barrages shook the ground, and as if that were not enough, the tanks located on the surrounding hills joined the fire. After the barrage, the Russian infantry (troops of 9th Infantry Brigade) launched their attack. It was supported by 12 tanks. As Martti had written in his diary, the Finnish companies were scattered all over the lines as support was needed in various points. After a whole day of fighting, the German troops held their ground and the Russians had to pull back. During these battles, the battalion lost four men (KIA) and 24 were wounded.

Rottenführer Martti Lehtonen – FFB/4.kp – Finnisches Freiwilligen Bataillon der Waffen SS/4. Kp.

The sound of incoming rounds were the prelude to another day of heavy fighting. At dawn the Russian forces resumed their attack, but this time they managed to tear up some holes in the German lines and for a while the Finnish 9th Company was fighting while surrounded by Russians who had managed to break through their flanks. After a fierce fight, the Russians were pushed back, but again it was paid for with lots of blood. On this day the battalion's ranks were further reduced: five killed and 13 wounded. Martti's company commander SS-Untersturmführer Heinz Walgenbach was killed in action and Martti had witnessed his death. Their positions were under mortar fire and Walgenbach was hit by shrapnel. Walgenbach was respected by his men, and he was one of those company commanders that Finns looked up to. Another Finnish volunteer stated after the war that SS-Ustuf Walgenbach was just starting to eat his ration when the barrage hit. Martti was appointed as a squad leader he same day. The Russians had also suffered enough losses that their assault started to lose its strength. During the next days, between October 12 and 13, the Russians tried to break the lines again but their weak efforts were futile.

Hill 701 was still one of the Germania Regiment's main objectives. On October 15, Battalion Diekmann (I/Germania) and Battalion Nickel (of the Wehrmacht's 70. Regiment) with support of four Sturmgeschütz assault guns, attacked Hills 694 and 701. Even with this amount of force the assault was halted. During the afternoon, the Finnish Battalion received orders to engage in the fight and help the troops that were already there. But it didn't make any difference. Only more men got killed (13 killed and 16 wounded). The Russians managed to maintain their lines and the assault was stopped before nightfall. Reinforcements were organized the next morning, and the Germans were again ready to make another push. The next day the Germans brought three battalions to the front lines (not in full fighting force because of the heavy losses), accompanied by tanks. It meant that it was now or never for Hill 701! With the support of armored vehicles and the soldiers showing ultimate courage under heavy fire, the Germans managed to conquer the Hill 701. On top of the hill, the exhausted Finnish soldiers were lying in the trenches surrounded by corpses of Russian soldiers. This was the most eastern and highest ground that the Finnish men reached in the whole war.

"Saturday October 17 – 1942: Another tough day. Maula and Ora arrived today but both got wounded. Berglund got killed. Ruskies are coming again. It is 1500h."

The Russians were not planning to give this hill up just like that. In the morning of October 17, thick mist provided cover for the Russian forces to move right up to the German lines. What followed was a close combat battle. Both sides were throwing hand grenades at each other, and company commanders Mühlinghaus and Pallesche were both badly wounded. Obersturmführer August Mühlinghaus later succumbed to his wounds. SS-Ostuf Pohjanlehto took command, and a little while later, SS-Obersturmführer Ertel took command of the 9th Company. The battalion had lost all of their artillery observers and there was only one signaler left who could operate a radio. The Germans had only a couple of tanks there, but those couldn't operate properly because the mist caused limited visibility. The battalion managed to halt the attack, and the remaining Russian troops retreated into the mist.

The Russians returned in the afternoon, and this time they brought four tanks to the front, and there was an entire battalion (almost 300 men) attacking the hill. However the Germans had already sent reinforcements to Hill 701 early in the morning. Five German tanks came to help, and managed to knock out two of the four Russian tanks. The Russian infantry advanced while under their

Rottenführer Martti Lehtonen – FFB/4.kp – Finnisches Freiwilligen Bataillon der Waffen SS/4. Kp.

artillery support. Their artillery was heavily shelling the positions on the hilltop. However the Finns and the Germans didn't take one step back, and the Russians didn't manage to throw them off the hill. Result: the Russians had to retreat again, and this time Hill 701 was conquered for good. Still the Russian forces tried again to attack the German positions on the hill, however they were stopped by heavy artillery fire before they could start their advance towards the hill. After the battle, it was easier to count those who were still alive, and the Finnish Battalion's combined strength of the 10th and 11th Companies was only one officer and 12 men! On October 19 they were pulled away from Hill 701, and it was left in the hands of Group Diekmann (I/Germania).

The Finnish Battalion occupied a new sector which wasn't near Malgobek at all. This sector was far from the focal point of the previous battles, and the men were tired and needed some well deserved rest. Martti had been seriously ill during the battles of Hill 701. Since October 18 the entries in his diary mentioned that he had been vomiting and that couldn't eat anything. But every man was needed for combat, so there was no time to rest. When the battalion took their new position it also had to report its fighting strength; on October 22 it consisted of nine officers, 56 NCOs and 164 men. The battalion remained in this sector until the end of October. They mainly fought trench wars during this time, and they didn't take part in any operation.

The operations in Malgobek were the Germans' last attempts to take the advantage in the Caucasus, and the Finnish Battalion was thrown into it without remorse. In 1942, the German war machine had already lost a lot of its power while the Russians were getting stronger every day with the help of their allies, of course. The German commanders tried to obey and fulfill Hitler's orders which meant a tremendous amount of losses. There weren't any reserves to replace those losses, and the shortage of fuel made the situation even worse. It was unfortunate for the Finnish volunteers to be there at that time.

In these battles of Malgobek, the Finnish Volunteer Battalion had lost 40% of its theoretical strength. The loss of the actual strength was 60%: in total six officers and 82 NCOs and regular troops were killed; 11 officers and 355 NCOs and troops were wounded. There were also 78 men that had been reported ill. All together the total casualties were 434 men. General Paavo Talvela from the Finnish Army visited the battalion on October 21 just after the Battle of Hill 701. Finnish Army commander Field Marshal Mannerheim gave general Talvela decorations to award some of the men. General Talvela took 20 Crosses of Liberty and 100 Medals of Liberty with him. When he arrived at the Malgobek front lines and saw the remnants of the battalion, he decided to give every medal he had. It was now a battalion only in name, not by its manpower!

Retreat from the Caucasus – Back to the Don

The Finnish Battalion switched their positions and moved to a village called Verhnij Kurp. The Germans anticipated a Russian attack on the northern sector of the River Terek, and they organized and prepared defensive positions. The transfer of the Finnish Battalion was part of these preparations. Verhnij Kurp was a quiet place, and the Finns mainly fortified their positions there and patrolled the area. The Finnish Battalion III/Nordland was pulled from the Malgobek front lines for the last time during the night of November 11–12. In Verhnij Kurp, Martti's condition worsened, and he had to be taken to a field hospital. He was vomiting again, couldn't eat anything, and there was blood in his feces. His hands and feet were swollen terribly. There weren't any doctors left that could diagnose his condition, but it is highly possible that he had dysentery.

Rottenführer Martti Lehtonen – FFB/4.kp – Finnisches Freiwilligen Bataillon der Waffen SS/4. Kp.

On November 10, Martti was transferred to Pavlovskaya, and from there all the way to Rostov by train. Martti arrived in Rostov on November 17. In Rostov, Martti's situation wasn't getting any better, and the doctors were constantly assessing his situation. It was decided that he must be transferred to Germany to get better treatment. On November 22 he left Rostov with a train that transported the sick and heavily wounded back to Germany. They travelled via Lublin to Döbeln where the train arrived on December 2, 1942. The hospital was in Döbeln where Martti's illness was treated for 17 days. Martti didn't write in his diary anymore after December 19, 1942. After that day, it is a bit uncertain where he was. Most likely, and what can be seen in few of his personal documents, is that Martti was sent back to Finland for convalescence. Martti had been in Graz at the beginning of 1943. Then in February 1943 Martti traveled to Finland, and came back to Germany in April. He wasn't sent to the front line anymore. He was in Ruhpolding in May when the Finnish Battalion was there as well. Martti came back to Finland with the other volunteers on June 1, 1943.

The German forces had seized Alagir in the beginning of November 1942. Alagir lies approximately 100 km south of Malgobek. The LII Army Group needed reinforcements in Alagir, and they ordered the Wiking Division to move from Malgobek to Alagir. The Finnish Battalion was transported to a village called Digora, and from there they continued to Dzuaryqaeu, east of Alagir. The battalion arrived at its position on November 14, and its objective was to defend the road that led to Alagir. The battalion stayed there for approximately 10 days. The enemy wasn't causing too much harm: some Russian patrols caused skirmishes, but the Finns didn't suffer any significant losses. The poor weather conditions actually caused more trouble than the Russians. These positions didn't have any reasonable shelter for the inclement weather, and the men had to sit in wet clothes with temperatures dropping below 0 degrees Celsius. The Finnish Battalion moved to the village of Karman-Sindzikau on November 24 where they met the men of the Finnish replacement company. The Finnish and German government had agreed on recruiting reinforcements, however Finnish officials limited the recruitment to 200 men, and they made a contract that would end at the same time as the battalion's contract. Two days earlier, General Steiner was ordered to take command of the III Panzer Army. This arrangement was temporary, and Steiner later returned to his post. The Wiking Division received a new commander since SS-Brigadeführer Herbert Otto Gille had taken command. Later Gille became the full time commander of the Wiking Division in May 1943.

After a short stay in Karman-Sindzikau, the battalion moved to Chikola. There they set up a defensive perimeter around the village, and one of the famous battles of the Finnish Battalion was fought there in Chikola. It was on the morning of December 4 when Russian forces attacked the village. Near the village was a river bank, and there the battalion had set up its defense. Six men armed with a machine gun manned that fortified position. They fought eight straight hours, and two of the men were killed and two were wounded. Only SS-Rottenführer Kalevi Könönen and SS-Schütze Yrjö Pyyhtiä were still standing and continued to fight. Their machine gun was out of ammo, and they had to shoot aimed single shots to spare ammunition. The Finnish counter-attack came at 1400h, and relieved these two poor men. By the time of the counter-attack there were over 200 dead Russians in front of their positions and another 200 Russians were taken prisoners. For this, both men received the Iron Cross First and Second Class (with the award document personally signed by Hitler), and their names were included in the Honor Roll of the German Army (the Ehrenblatt des deutschen

Rottenführer Martti Lehtonen – FFB/4.kp – Finnisches Freiwilligen Bataillon der Waffen SS/4. Kp.

Heeres). They later also received an Ehrenspange (Honor Roll Clasp) of the Iron Cross.

In November 1942, the Russian forces had already completed Operation Uranus, the encirclement of German forces in Stalingrad. The Russian success in Stalingrad caused pressure on Army Group A's forces in the Caucasus. The Russian Army was already making preparations for Operation Saturn which aimed to cut off Army Group A in the Caucasus. The German forces were still bravely fighting in Stalingrad which gave Army Group A the time to reorganize their forces and to start the withdrawal from the Caucasus. By the end of December 1942, Hitler had given orders to the 1st Panzer Army to withdraw its forces from the Caucasus. At that time the Finnish Battalion was in the Middle Caucasus, positioned in the villages of Toldsgun and Hasnidon. The battalion received its marching orders and they started packing on New Year's Eve. They left the villages during the night. This didn't go unnoticed by the Russians, and they started to chase the battalion. After quite intense firefight, the battalion managed to get rid of their pursuers. The battalion drove six days in snow storms and freezing temperatures.

On January 6, 1943, they arrived in Stavropol. The fuel supply was cut off, and they were forced to stay three days in Stavropol. On January 9, they continued north while driving over the Kalmykian plains. During the first two days they managed to drive more than 240 km. The Army Group commanders sent the Wiking Division to support General Hoth's 4th Panzer Army in its fight on the River Kuberle front. The Finnish Battalion arrived there on January 12 and stayed as a reserve.

On January 14, Russian forces entered the village of Krasnoye Znamya. With 8 tanks and 400 men they managed to push the Germans back. The 11th Company of the Finnish Battalion was ordered to join I/Nordland and to take part in a counter-attack. After two days of fighting the Russian troops were thrown out of the village for good. During the first day of the battle, the Russians had lost 200 men (KIA) and the Finns had only two killed and 13 wounded. The village of Krasnoye Znamya was approximately 300 km south of Stalingrad, and it was the closest place that the Finns ever got to Stalingrad.

The Finnish Battalion was now in Shabliyevka, just south of Krasnoye Znamya. From there they were ordered on January 19 to move to the village of Yekaterinovka (Ekaterinovka). The men were loaded onto trucks, and they were driven to their new location at the break of dawn. On the way there, the men saw a couple of new Tiger panzers for the first time. This new Tiger tank and its capabilities had already acquired some reputation among the troops, and the Finns had also heard stories about this new panzer. After the arrival in Yekaterinovka, the battalion was attached to SR 40 (Schützen-Regiment 40). The Germans had spotted a strong enemy force in the nearby village and reconnaissance had estimated that there were almost 1000 men with heavy weapons and mortars in the village. The attack on the village began at 0900h. At first the German troops literally overran the first Russian positions. SS-Hauptsturmführer Porsch, commander of 10th Company, was sitting on top of a moving tank and leading the attack when he was killed. He was shot straight through the head. After Porsch was killed, SS-Ostuf Pohjanlehto took command. The German assault wasn't moving forwards anymore because the defenders managed to reset their defensive lines. Just as it seemed that the battalion would get pinned down they got help from above. Nine Stukas with their sirens screaming dropped their bombs on the Russian positions. The rage of the heavens! After all of the Stukas had dropped their bombs, they continued to strafe some targets in the village. The Germans tried to

Rottenführer Martti Lehtonen – FFB/4.kp – Finnisches Freiwilligen Bataillon der Waffen SS/4. Kp.

take advantage of the chaos created by the Stukas. After withdrawing, the Russian forces redeployed and counter-attacked: a Soviet unit of 600 men attacked SS-Ostuf Pohjanlehto's company's positions. Wave after wave of Russian soldiers charged the German lines. The Finns stayed in their positions and fired their machine guns so hard that the barrels almost melted! After a while, another large Soviet attack wave came. The defenders quickly estimated that it was most likely a unit comprised of 400 men. With a stubborn defense, these attacks were repelled time after time, and in the afternoon all Russian counter-attacks had been successfully defended. The aftermath of that day's battle for the battalion was one officer, three NCOs, and five men killed; five NCOs and 19 men had been wounded.

The main perimeter of the village was occupied by the Germans, and the Russian forces were pushed to the northern end of the village. The next morning on January 20, the Sturmgeschütz assault guns came to support the attack. The Russians were completely caught by surprise, and with the support of the artillery and Sturmgeschütze, the Germans managed to throw out the rest of the enemy forces from the village. The Russian forces tried again to counter-attack, and charged in open terrain. Two Soviet units, one about 100 men, and another of about 300 men, were charging from the east and southeast. It was a desperate attempt, but they finally had to retreat when they faced heavy resistance from the village. The battalion lost five NCOs and 13 men wounded on the last two days of the battle. This victory was obviously a huge morale boost for the Finns. They had beaten an enemy which was almost seven times stronger in manpower. The battalion had been reduced to only a handful of men, but those men proved that they had become skilled, battle tested, hard fighting soldiers. In Yekaterinovka, the battalion took many prisoners. Those prisoners reported that they were soldiers of the 9th Infantry Brigade, and that their objective was to take control of the road to Proletarsk. The German forces in Proletarsk would have been cut off had the Russians succeeded. The Finnish Battalion had won precious time for the other units to continue their withdrawal.

On January 24, Hitler had given orders that the 1st Panzer Army would withdraw to Rostov-on-Don. It was the only way out. This literally meant that the entire 1st Panzer Army would go through Rostov. The Finnish Battalion was retreating towards Rostov. During the withdrawal, both sides needed shelter as neither of them wanted to stay overnight in snow and freezing temperatures. This is one of the reasons why both sides fought hard to control local villages. The battalion was nearly surrounded in Zelina on January 23, but after heavy fighting they managed to push through the enemy lines. Finally on February 4, the Finnish Battalion arrived in Rostov. It's hard to imagine the sight in Rostov when all units of the army group were making their way forward by using just one lane. But there was only one way across the River Don, and it was the power plant dam near the city. The Finnish Battalion waited for two days before it could cross the river. Some units of the battalion already had crossed the river on February 4, but the rest of the battalion only managed to cross the river on February 7. This was called "the greatest traffic jam in the world". Some Finns witnessed an episode where a truck broke down right in the middle of the dam and the whole line stopped. A German officer came swiftly to the site and after a quick negotiation, the truck was pushed off the dam and the line was moving again. The river was frozen in some parts, so the infantry could walk across it. After crossing the river there were different signs posted for each particular unit, and the direction they had to follow. That way the flow of traffic wasn't stopped on the other side. Somehow the Germans succeeded, and managed to move their 1st and 4th Panzer Armies into safety on time. After the Finnish Battalion was on the other side of the Don, it headed north. Their next destination was the city of Gorlovka (Horlivka). En route to Gorlovka, they drove through some familiar places from the previous winter: Uspenskaya and Amvrosievka. In Uspenskaya there was a military cemetery where many of their fallen comrades had been buried, and it was in Amvrosievka where the battalion was welcomed to the front lines by General Steiner. The city of Gorlovka was 50 km north of Stalino, and the battalion arrived there on February 11.

One More Push to the East - the Finnish Battalion's Last Battles

The Russian Army's high command had launched Operation Gallop at end of January. This operation was conducted by the Russian Army's Southwestern Front (an army front was the equivalent force of a German Army Group), commanded by General Nikolai Vatutin. The goal of the operation was to push towards the Sea of Azov and cut off all the German forces east of Donetsk. General Popov's large tank formations stormed through the weakened German lines. In this situation the German high command formed the Army Group South which consisted of the remnants of Army Groups A, B, and Army Group Don, and it was put under the command of Field Marshal Erich von Manstein.

The Wiking Division was now part of the XXXX Panzer Corps commanded by General Heinrici. Popov's tanks had reached the city of Krasnoarmeiskoye by February 10, and General Heinrici ordered the Wiking Division to move quickly to Krasnoarmeiskoye and strengthen the city defenses. During the early hours of the next morning, the Finnish Battalion was on the move again. The Nordland Regiment, accompanied by the Finnish Battalion, was in position when they hit the Russian lines just south of Krasnoarmeiskoye near the village of Novo Pavlovka. The men jumped off the trucks and rushed into battle. The battalion received orders to take the village, which it did after almost three days of heavy fighting. During that time, the village changed hands three times. Russian forces managed to take the village twice before the Nordland Regiment managed to push them back out.

On February 21, the XXXX Panzer Army was now attacking the city from almost every direction, and managed to encircle it. The Wiking Division was attacking from the south when Popov requested permission to retreat which was refused by the upper command. The Finnish Battalion didn't take part in the fighting in the city center, and they were spared from the bloodiest part of this urban warfare as the Germans entered the city. However, the battalion fought their way to the city through the suburbs. The Finns reached the south side train station first, which was just on the outskirts of the city. Some of the Russian troops managed to retreat, but there were enough Russians left behind so that the hostilities in the city continued until February 24. The Wiking Division was pulled out of the city between February 21-22. The Finnish Battalion subsequently moved to the city of Slavyanka for couple days of well deserved rest.

The Russian Army's Southwestern Front had stubbornly denied any retreat, and pushed their attack even when it impossible. The Russians had already miscalculated the German readiness and capabilities to perform offensive maneuvers, and Popov's mobile units were cut off, and supply lines were struggling to get fuel to the tanks. Manstein had launched several offensives to capture Kharkov, and the German forces were advancing again. This was the last time that the Finnish Battalion took part in a large motorized offensive. The battalion advanced almost 200 km between February 24 and March 4. The battles in between were mainly village skirmishes. They arrived at the southern banks of the River Donets just west of Izjum, located 120 km southeast of Kharkov. These positions were the last ones for the Finnish Battalion. On March 1, 1943, the battalion reported that its fighting strength was reduced to only eight officers, 37 NCOs, and 192 men. The whole situation stabilized into a trench war, but both sides started to prepare for rasputitsa season, and there weren't any more major battles in the Finnish sector. The battalion stayed in this sector from March 4 to April 10.

A group of well-armed Finnish volunteers in a Ukrainian village - spring 1943.

Back Home - Honorably Discharged

Discussions about the situation of the Finnish Battalion had already started in February 1943. Finnish and German officials had been negotiating the battalion's future. There were also plans to expand the battalion to a full-sized regiment, but it was never pushed through. The Germans decided to start the preparations for the demobilization of the Finnish Battalion. The whole Wiking Division would be reorganized in April anyway, and the Finnish Battalion was replaced at the front by the 457. Grenadier Regiment on April 10, and the battalion was sent far behind the lines. Before that, on April 14, the Finns handed their weapons over to the Estonian SS-Battalion in Narva. The Estonians had arrived at the front immediately after their training, and they were attached to the Wiking Division.

The Finnish Battalion was discharged from the Wiking Division on April 24. General Steiner thanked the men and also Heinrich Himmler personally came to say his farewells to the Finnish volunteers. After two weeks of rest, the battalion was transported to Germany by train where it arrived in Grafenwöhr on May 7. Grafenwöhr was near Nürnberg, and there was also an army training center. The rest of the Finns that were in replacement and convalescent companies in Graz were also transported to Grafenwöhr. It was a joyful reunion as many men saw their comrades again after a long time. The recovering wounded men were also present. It is quite possible that it was in Grafenwöhr when Martti rejoined the battalion. From Grafenwöhr, they were all sent to Bavaria. The train arrived in the idyllic town of Rupohlding which was a vacation center in the Bavarian Alps. There the battalion got two more weeks of rest and relaxation. On May 23, they held a parade (the men got rifles for the parade) and then there was a big celebration in the evening at the local festhall Kurhaus. SS-Gruppenführer Steiner was present, and he gave a speech, followed by singing, dancing, and drinking. After that, the men prepared for their trip back to their homeland. There was one particular phrase that they wrote on the trains: *"Räder müssen rollen, das wir nach Hause kommen!"* The Battalion left Ruhpolding between May 23 and 28. From Ruhpolding, the troops were transported by train to Tallinn in Estonia. On the night of May 31, the battalion was at the harbor of Tallinn, and early in the morning all the men were aboard the S/S Warthe. The docks of the harbor of Hanko were empty, and only three officers were standing on the quay. "We left in silence and we returned in silence" one volunteer wrote in his diary. Their commander SS-Gruppenführer Steiner had also arrived in Finland,

Rottenführer Martti Lehtonen – FFB/4.kp – Finnisches Freiwilligen Bataillon der Waffen SS/4. Kp.

and Steiner presided over the battalion's parade in Hanko. Notable members of the Finnish Army and state officials were missing. The commander of home front troops, General Malmberg, was the highest ranking Finnish officer present at the parade. The Finnish government and the high command of Finnish Army had started to differentiate themselves from Nazi-Germany. That's why they kept a low profile upon the battalion's return. Even the original plan was that the battalion would arrive in Finland's capital Helsinki, but officials changed the port of arrival to Hanko. The battalion had a homecoming ceremony in Tampere on June 3. Newspapers wrote about it, and radio broadcasters interviewed some of the battalion's men. The arrival wasn't kept completely secret. Censorship assured that news about the battalion's return was kept very formal. After the ceremony, the battalion was granted a one month leave. After that, the men were ordered to return to Hanko were they would get new orders about the next phase.

Disbandment of the Battalion and Transfer to the Finnish Army

Finland's government had been in a difficult situation since early 1943. After the Germans had suffered a major defeat in Stalingrad, it seemed clear that Finland had to steer its way out of the war. The Finnish government had contacted the Soviet foreign ministry in February to seek the possibility of peace talks. These actions were not kept secret from the Germans, and it caused a diplomatic break-up, and the Germans halted much needed material and food help to Finland. So it was a very fragile situation as to how to answer in a correct and polite way to the Germans that the battalion's contract wasn't going to be extended. Field Marshal Mannerheim made his move and took responsibility of the battalion's future. Field Marshal Mannerheim wrote a memo to Hitler. In this memo, Mannerheim explained that Finnish Army would need these men. It wasn't the answer Waffen SS organization wanted, and it caused some dismay.

Germania's Assault Generation

At this point, Hitler had his focus solely on the events on the Eastern Front. Hitler accepted Mannerheim's proposal on July 4.

While diplomatic games were played in the background, the men had been waiting in Hanko for something to happen. Rumors spread, and men became very frustrated. Finally on July 7, the order came that battalion would be disbanded. This news upset the men, but the situation was handled with great diplomacy. On July 11, the battalion had a ceremony where the battalion's commander Collani gave a speech. Collani awarded 45 Iron Crosses, and shook every man's hand as a goodbye. Straight after the ceremony, the men went to the barracks and were dressed in Finnish uniforms. Then they were gathered again and the senior officer saluted General Malmberg and reported the battalion on duty. Germans weren't allowed to join in this part of the ceremony. Many of the battalion's men were sent to officer courses. A total of 303 men became officers in the Finnish Army. The Finnish Armored Division (Finnish: Panssaridivisioona, Ps.D) was one of those units where many of the former volunteers served at the Finnish Front. During the hostilities on the Finnish Front, 113 former volunteers had lost their lives. Finland reached an armistice with Russia on September 19, 1944. One of the conditions of the armistice was that Finland had to expel all German troops from its territory. The Germans weren't leaving, and the Russians pushed Finland to take action. The so called Lapland War broke out as the Finns fought their co-belligerents in Lapland. The former volunteers weren't ordered to take part in this, but some went and fought. Three of the battalion's men were killed in those battles.

Martti was ordered to the 12th Field Artillery Regiment, where he attained the rank of corporal. This field artillery regiment was attached to the 15th Infantry Division. The 15th Division was at the Karelian Isthmus front. There in the front lines, Martti met his future wife. She was there doing volunteer work as a Lotta. In Finland there

Rottenführer Martti Lehtonen – FFB/4.kp – Finnisches Freiwilligen Bataillon der Waffen SS/4. Kp.

was an auxiliary paramilitary organization for women called, "Lotta Svärd". These "Lottas" volunteered and worked in various assignments. They got married in March 1944.

Martti took part in the bloody battles at the Karelian Front. Russians started one of their strategic offensives in June. The Leningrad Front had gathered significant force against Finland. Martti fought in the Battle of Äyräpää-Vuosalmi, where the outnumbered Finnish forces managed to repel the Russian assault causing heavy losses to the Russian Army units. Almost 60,000 Russians with 150 tanks tried cross the River Vuoksi. The Finns had 30,000 men and 35 assault guns at their disposal. After almost two weeks of fighting, the Russians had lost over 3000 men killed in action, and the number of wounded ranged somewhere between 9,000 - 11,000 men. The Russian Army couldn't break through the Finnish lines, and the defenders held their positions until the end of the war.

After the war, Martti settled in Pori. There he opened a small shop where he sold bags and suitcases. He and his wife had five kids. Martti kept in contact with his comrades after the war. The Finnish Secret Police was watching over the Finnish volunteers after the war. They had to keep low profile after the war. As time went by and things started to change, the local Waffen SS veterans in Pori started meeting regularly once every month. These meetings were held in the same restaurant for years. Martti regularly took part in these meetings. Martti Lehtonen died on September 25, 1961 in Pori.

Closing Words

The Finnish Waffen SS Volunteer Battalions, comprised of 1400 men, were just a tiny piece of a great German Army of millions of men during WWII. In Finnish history however, the volunteer battalion is one of those major factors that still defines the connection to Nazi-Germany. Finland's role alongside Nazi-Germany is still a highly debated topic: were they allies by terms, or was their faith bonded to Germany because they had the same enemy? The battalion was recruited by the Finns and not by the Germans! The Finnish government gave acceptance for it, and it was a government project that was controlled by the Ministry of Foreign Affairs and the army's high command. The Battalion was also a sign of trust and co-operation towards Germany. It was also a special kind of battalion within the Waffen SS. Finnish volunteers came from a country that wasn't occupied by Germans. It was also apolitical, and there weren't any political figures in the background. The Finnish Volunteer Battalion even got its own Finnish military chaplain which was a rare feature in the non-religious Waffen SS. After the war, the Finnish government changed their attitude towards the former Waffen SS volunteers even though most of them served in the Finnish Army after their return from Germany. As communist parties won the elections, the Finnish volunteers were under surveillance. Many of them were arrested by the newly organized secret police and interrogated, but no one pressed charges against these men. In some workplaces, the background of Waffen SS service was taken so heavily that some men quit their job and looked for other career opportunities. None of the Finns were put on trial or accused of war crimes. It is clear that the SS was a stigma, and after the war when all the atrocities were revealed, it grew even bigger. Many of the Finnish volunteers still managed to work their way up despite their SS background. One of those was the battalion's Ustuf Sulo Suorttanen, who served as Minister of Defense from 1966 to 1970. It will stay forever unclear what Martti really thought about the choice he had made. His relatives had said that he wasn't very pleased how things went in Germany, but he had signed the contract, like everyone else, and he was living up to his promise and oath. After the war he never talked about the war or what he had seen or done. Sometimes after a

Rottenführer Martti Lehtonen – FFB/4.kp – Finnisches Freiwilligen Bataillon der Waffen SS/4. Kp.

few beers he would say something or maybe sing a German marching song. He had told his brother that it was a terrible journey, but at least he was lucky to have survived the ordeal. Whatever the situation was or how bad it was, they had to get things done. They were loyal to the man next to them, and followed their orders as best they possibly could.

SS-Rottenführer Martti Lehtonen with his girlfriend during home coming leave in Finland - June 1943.

From the Frw. Standarte Nordwest to the Germanic SS in Flanders

The media always portrayed us as SS monsters. When you say "SS man" that's something I can live, with but calling us, calling me, an SS monster that's completely absurd. Actually it's a straight lie! In May 1940, the Blitzkrieg ran through Belgium; I was only 18 years old at that time. I didn't know too much about Hitler at that time or the Third Reich. I had absolutely no interest in politics. My interest in Germany came when the Belgian government tried to send every young man between the age of 16 and 35 to the south of France. However, we didn't get any further than Boulogne-sur-Mere because the spearhead of the German panzer troops under Guderian were a lot faster than us. In Boulogne-sur-Mere there was still some resistance from the Belgian and French troops, but they were no match against this new German Army, the elite SS units who were forming the lead of the spearhead during the attacks. In the north of France I witnessed the mass capitulation of the Allies. A large group of French soldiers surrendered to a German NCO who had a particular sign on one of his collar tabs of his uniform: the double sieg rune or SS. The NCO and a couple of his men all had these lightning bolts on their uniform, and I had never seen that before. I had seen Heer soldiers before, and Luftwaffe, and Kriegsmarine, but I've never had seen these soldiers before. When I saw these lightning bolts, the SS runes on their uniform, something in me changed that I can't really explain. I was drawn to it, and I thought at that moment that there was something more behind the SS runes on the uniforms. The meeting with those SS soldiers changed the course of my life significantly. Back then lots of us were almost like hypnotized by the appearance of those German soldiers.

From the Frw. Standarte Nordwest to the Germanic SS in Flanders

When we had to make a choice between the poorly equipped Belgian Army on their camel boots, and the German Army with these Feldgrau uniforms, we immediately knew which to choose. I was so mesmerized by these uniforms, by their appearance they had. When I got back home in Belgium, I told my mother immediately about what I'd seen and how I felt about it. It was then that I told her that I had made the decision to follow the National-Socialists. I was the oldest of five children, and my parents were working in the diamond sector. My parents knew they had to leave me be in the decisions that I made. Yes I showed sympathies for the Germans, and I certainly didn't hide it from my family and friends. My parents never thought of me as being a collaborator. Why did I have to stay loyal to Flanders? For me it meant nothing anymore. My parents understood my point of view on the political situation at that time there is a reason why they allowed all their other children to join the Hitlerjugend. Even my father went to work for the Germans!

Joining the Waffen SS

When I decided to join the Waffen SS, I went to see my boss, the general manager of the Grand Bazar, Mr. Gyselinck, and I told him that I was joining the Waffen SS. I had to say this in French to him because he couldn't speak or understand Dutch! Mr. Gyselinck jumped out of his chair and yelled: "Get out of my office!" In September 1940, I reported to the Waffen SS – the SS-Freiwilligen Standarte Westland - but for the elitarian SS, the conditions to get recruited were very strict. I reported at the recruiting office on the Mechelsesteenweg in Antwerp – "*zaal Gruter*" – where I was confronted with a doctor, a Hauptsturmführer, who ordered me to do twenty genuflections. But I wasn't able to do that without pain because of an old injury I had on one of my knees. The Hauptsturmführer said to come back another time, and I was devastated because of that! I took a deep breath and told myself to be patient until my next appointment with the SS doctor. In the meantime, I joined the "Algemeene SS Vlaanderen" which was a perfect copy of the German SS. The Algemeene SS Vlaanderen was there for those who didn't want to join the Vlaams Nationalistisch Verbond or Flemish National League under Staf De Clercq, the Verbond van Dietsche Nationaal-Solidaristen (Verdinaso or Dinaso), or a similar nationalist group. Actually the Algemeene SS Vlaanderen was there for the ones that didn't trust these nationalist organizations. The VNV became the largest nationalist party in Flanders, but the SS didn't trust them at all. The Flemish SS formations had to provide men who would form the future leaders of a new Flemish Nazi Party.

The first thing we had to do was to swear an oath to the Führer. The VNV refused to swear an oath to the Führer because they swore loyalty to Staf De Clercq. The VNV was a bit too relaxed for us in how they managed things; their approach to things in life were more, let's say, romantic and more in the spirit of the old Flemish values. These old Flemish values were based on protests, but never on actions/reactions. For us it was different as we actually wanted to change something. We wanted to change society. In 1941, I finally received my call to the Waffen SS - the SS-Freiwilligen Standarte Nordwest - and together with a couple of comrades, I left for Germany. I was so proud! We were the first formation who made their way to the train station. A group of Dutch comrades joined us on the same day; they came from The Hague in The Netherlands. In Germany, we were all united in Hamburg in the Regiment "Nordwest" of the Waffen SS. We were stationed in the training camp of Langenhorn where all Western Europeans received their basic training for the Waffen SS. We went through a Spartan regime and training was very hard. But we were the elite! Next to the training camp there was a police station and every morning the police officers were watching us practicing the *"Gewehrgriff"*. This rifle drill was so perfect that we could've easily be compared to the Leibstandarte Adolf Hitler and we were all very proud of this!

Recruits of the Nordwest in Hamburg in 1941.

Going to the Front...

We knew that we had to go to the Eastern Front sooner or later, but we didn't know where we would end up at the front, in which sector, city, or town. We had absolutely no idea to which Abschnitt we were supposed to go. We were moved to the east, to Debica in Poland, to prepare us for the move to the front. More Flemings arrived in Debica, but none of these soldiers were involved in politics in the homeland. Except for the three Flemish officers: Jef Francois (Dinaso), Paul Suys (Rex), and Raymond Tollenaere (VNV – Zwarte Brigade or Black Brigade). Those three officers marched in front of us and while we were marching we looked at each other and said: "Look, those are our guys!" While we were in Debica, the group of Flemings got split up into two groups: there were the ones who refused to take the oath to Hitler but instead they swore allegiance to Staf De Clercq; and then you had the ones that swore allegiance to the Führer. I didn't want anything to do with those Staf De Clercq followers, and yes I looked down on these VNV members. I had absolutely no respect for them, and lots of the non-VNV members were always singing songs about the VNV portraying them as traitors and cowards. Simply said: they were people that you couldn't trust at all!

I went to the front in September 1941. I was only 19 years old and the first thing I did when I arrived at the front was to shoot a Russian soldier through his skinny body. I shot him not because I was a cold blooded killer, but because he was charging at me pointing his rifle in my direction. I shot him from a very close distance, but that day it was him or me that wouldn't go home. I was faster that day and I killed him. Yes one could have pity on that Russian soldier…you could even cry about what happened to him. But I didn't do that at all. Actually none of us did. At that moment we weren't human anymore, we had no feelings anymore. We were just like ghosts…

Close to Leningrad there was a wall in the middle of the terrain where we were fighting. But this was not a regular brick wall as we all know it. This wall was mostly built out of bodies, especially Russians. Inside the wall you could see skulls, bones, uniforms, boots…all what you could imagine about dead bodies…dead soldiers. I experienced myself that you couldn't lean against this wall as you would fall into it and come face to face with a skull. It was there at the Leningrad Front that my good friend Marcel died in my arms. While we, the infantry, were positioned in craters who were created earlier that day or during the previous days by an artillery barrage, our artillery began shelling the Russian positions. At least we thought they did. But because they miscalculated the Russian positions they shelled our positions instead. Because of this friendly fire my good friend Marcel had a very short life. An artillery shell hit him right in the head. After

From the Frw. Standarte Nordwest to the Germanic SS in Flanders

the war I told his parents that their son had died in combat which made it a lot easier for them to process the loss of their son. But for me it was a nightmare that continued my entire life! If they only had known that their son died because of the miscalculations of a Knight's Cross recipient to be...

In the church of Poperesky, the cigarette butts were laying on the altar while red colored helmets were laying all spread out on the church floor. Immediately we realized we weren't the first visitors to this church. We stayed overnight in the church, and while we were sleeping on hay sacks, the alarm went off and I heard someone yell my name. I jumped up and literally flew over all the sleeping soldiers on the ground. I went outside as I could hear an ambulance with a running engine, ready to depart to the field hospital. I recognized the voice. It was my brother who had also joined the Waffen SS and who was laying inside that ambulance. I was confused and scared; first they told me he was killed in action, and then I was told he was still alive. I honestly didn't know what or who to believe anymore. That moment I heard my brother calling my name, I broke down and started crying. I felt lost. A couple of days ago I was told that my brother was dead and now he was laying inside the ambulance still alive. He was in serious conditions as part of his leg was blown off. This moment at the front had a huge impact on my future existence and that's all I want to say about it.

In May 1942, I was sent to the officer school in Bad Tölz. I already won the Iron Cross First Class, and my superiors had noticed that I had leadership qualities. I have to say that I was happy and proud to become a leader, but it had to be earned. For me this was one of the most precious possessions. One day the Reichsführer-SS Himmler visited the school in Bad Tölz, and I thought now it's the time to talk to him. I was going to ask him what he thought about the situation in the east. "Reichsführer, werden wir der Krieg jetzt gewinnen?" - losing the war was something impossible! "Once we win this war what will happen to all of us?" And Himmler replied: "It's very simple. We would work with Stützpunkten which are Waffen SS formations surrounded by the Wehrmacht and Russians who are with us. Between these Stützpunkten there would be 200-300 km in between."

Becoming the Leader of the SS in Flanders

When I was 22 years old, I was made a leader of the SS in Flanders (Belgium). First I thought that I would have to go back to the Russian Front after graduation, but things turned out differently for me. Instead I was made leader of the Algemeene SS Vlaanderen (later known as the *Germaansche SS Vlaanderen*) by the top of the SS. I was appointed by Himmler, Obergruppenführer Berger, and by Dr. van de Wiele. Berger and Dr. van de Wiele were in a meeting with Himmler when he asked them in his Bavarian dialect: "Für die Germanische-SS, was machen wir damit?" Berger and van de Wiele looked at each other and replied to Himmler: "We have the right candidate, Reichsführer." – "Who is it?" asked Himmler. Berger and van de Wiele mentioned my name but the only issue they had was my age. Obviously I was very young for a leader's position but Himmler said: "That's OK. Is he able to do that job or not?" to which both men replied "Yes he is the perfect candidate!" – "Then the job is his!" replied Himmler.

When I was on my post in Belgium as the new leader of the Germaansche SS (Germanic SS), I was asked to be very severe towards the resistance. The resistance started to take more actions against the German Army, and they had to be stopped at all costs. While at a funeral of a collaborator at the cemetery of Langemarck, where all my men were lined up, I swore that whoever would kill one of us or sympathizers of the regime would be waiting the same destiny!

Germaansche SS Vlaanderen – Meir, Antwerp.

The first action of the Germaansche SS took place in February 1944 with the objective a raid on the police station in the suburb of Vorst by Brussels. The police station was located in the Wielemans-Ceuppenslaan, and I demanded that all my staff members would be present during the raid. Three people were killed that day at the police station: two police officers and one civilian who was suspected to be a resistance fighter. I don't call it murder, but an execution and I have absolutely no regrets about what happened there. Yes it was a shame of those two innocent police officers who had nothing to do with the resistance, but during the commotion at the police station they were caught in the line of fire. Many other raids would follow. My task was as the leader to the Germaansche SS was to put my men at the disposition of the safety corps which was created by van de Wiele. Our actions had to be hard and effective. The Germans didn't respond to the violence committed against them because they were lazy! We had to maintain the safety of all!

We had to organize raids especially in those towns where it was suspected that there would be lots of resistance fighters. Meensel-Kiezegem is an example of those raids. Several civilians were killed, and more than sixty people were arrested and deported to the concentration camps - only six came back. That the others wouldn't come back from the camps, that I didn't know. I witnessed how these people were loaded onto trucks and then I realized that most likely the majority of them had nothing to do with the resistance. I wasn't having second thoughts, but it kind of hit me in a certain way. I walked towards the trucks, and I apologized to the first man that was sitting there.

When the Allies landed in Normandy in 1944, I gave the order to evacuate. The resistance became more and more active after the landings. When we left our headquarters in Brussels, all of a sudden you'd see only Belgian tri-color armbands outside on the street. Before that I had never seen them, but now there were thousands of them and they were eagerly distributed in the streets. The Germans evacuated first, but I had one task to complete in my headquarters. We had to burn numerous documents: files, papers, maps, etc. I burned them all, or most of them, with the help of three police officers. The courthouse in Brussels had to go, we wanted to burn it down to the ground with everything that was inside. Most likely there were thousands of files inside the courthouse which had to be destroyed before we left. After the evacuation, I became the military

From the Frw. Standarte Nordwest to the Germanic SS in Flanders

advisor of van de Wiele. The reason why is because he didn't know where to go or what to do between all these German soldiers. So he asked me to take care of business. We established a headquarters in the castle of Termont, and it was there where I met Cyriel Verschaeve, a priest. Not that I was that religious, but I wanted to talk to him about what I felt inside. Not that I had any remorse, but I wanted to let the priest know that in some situations I was forced to do things that were morally not acceptable. We walked through the park of the castle and I asked him: "What is my fault in all of this?" He simply replied that I had nothing to fear and that I shouldn't feel bad. "Only God will judge you sooner or later."

The End

We always believed in the final victory, and the reason why is because we always heard people talk about the "special" or "super" weapons the Germans had. These were, obviously, the V-weapons. We didn't only have the duty to obey, but we also believed what we were told. We always believed the Führer when he told us in the earlier stages of the war that he would engage the V-weapons which would kill every single Allied soldier! When we figured out that the end of the Reich was near, we made up our minds on how we would handle the situation. I reported myself for a suicide mission: these missions were manned torpedoes that were fired towards enemy ships. The pilot of the torpedo would make sure to direct the torpedo into the ship, and then blow himself up during impact. But when I reported for the mission, I got a firm "Nein!" because non-Germans were not allowed to take part in these missions. After the capitulation, I was captured almost immediately and I was tried as a SS monster. I spent three years on death row, but I was one of the last prisoners to be set free after spending 16 years in prison. I think they kept me that long in prison because they thought I would get killed by the *"Witte Brigade"* or White Brigade which were one of the resistance groups in Belgium. They killed numerous people after the war, so maybe it was a good thing that I spent a fair amount of years in prison. Of course the world changed a lot after 16 years. At the last moment, before I was granted my freedom back, the prime minister in Belgium said to me before he left his office: "The elite of this country stood on your side during the war, not on ours!"

I know that a lot of my comrades, that a lot of Waffen SS soldiers, tried to hide their SS past because they were ashamed to have belonged to this organization. I can only say, several decades after the war, that if it ever comes to a farewell I can only say these words: "Trotz allem bleibt meine Ehre Treue!" ("Despite everything, my honor remains faithful.")

Schwerer Granatwerfer Zug – 4.Kp/I. Btl/67. Rgt/III. SS-Panzer-Korps

Before I start with my personal story, I want to give you some information about the formation of the "Legion Flandern" and the "27.SS-Freiwilligen-Grenadier-Division Langemarck." After the occupation of the Netherlands and Belgium by the Germans in May 1940, the Reichsführer SS Heinrich Himmler started to recruit foreign volunteers to reinforce his newly established SS Regiment "Westland". First they wanted to use the Westland for policing activities and operations in the occupied areas, but soon, when the regiment was complete, it was integrated into the "Wiking" Division. On April 3, 1941, encouraged by this recruiting success, a new SS Regiment was created named "Nordwest" which consisted also of Danish volunteers. The Nordwest was going to be used for the same purpose as the Westland. Shortly after the invasion of Russia in June 1941, a new legion was created, the Flemish Legion or "Vlaams Legioen" which also had to fight against the Bolsheviks. Lots of members of the Nordwest were prepared to join this fight on the Eastern Front, and every young man between 17 and 40 years of age was more than welcome to enlist. Former officers of the Belgian Army were especially welcomed with open arms. On August 8, 1941, approximately 405 Flemish volunteers marched in front of the Palais des Beaux Arts to receive their banner. For their training, they were sent to the "Militärlager" in Debica in Poland which was very close to Krakow. There they met up with former volunteers of the Regiment Nordwest and by the end of September, 875 Flemings were sent to the Eastern Front. The officers were unfortunately all Germans.

Germania's Assault Generation

In 1941, the Legion was engaged at the Leningrad Front for the first time as part of the 2.SS-Infanterie-Brigade. During violent fighting in temperatures sinking as low as -40 degrees Celsius, the Legion sustained many casualties, especially because the winter started very early that year – somewhere in October. Until May 31, 1943, the Legion saw action on the Eastern Front until they were reorganized into the 6.Freiwilligen-Sturmbrigade Langemarck (under Konrad Schellong). By October 18, 1944, they became the 27.SS-Freiwiligen Grenadier Division (attached to the III. SS-Panzer Korps under the command of SS-Oberf. Thomas Müller). During the retreat from the Eastern Front, the division lost approximately 75% of its men! The last battles were fought near Prenzlau. From there the division was dissolved, and the members were given civilian clothing and started marching westwards to stay out of Russian captivity. The majority of the members were taken prisoner on May 10, 1945 near Schwerin by the English forces.

The majority of the Flemish volunteers were returned to Belgium where they were handed over to the Belgian authorities. They were seen as collaborators and lots of them were tried during mock/show trials, they were mistreated, and they were sentenced to the death penalty. The death penalty was usually never executed, but they kept these young men in captivity for a very long time. They were released after they served their time in prison, but society made it quite difficult for them. They had no rights, and it was not easy to find a job because they were seen as traitors. Many of them decided to return to Germany where they were able to lead a normal life. The psychological humiliation by their own state haunted them for many decades after the war, however they never lost their love for their Fatherland, and until today this love is still passionate and strong in their hearts.

Schwerer Granatwerfer Zug - 4.Kp/I. Btl/67. Rgt/III. SS-Panzer Korps

I was born on January 24, 1923, and I was the youngest of three boys. My brothers were respectively 16 and 18 years older than me. My father (born in 1880) was an architect and contractor who mostly built bridges. He was also politically engaged, and he was a member of the Parliament of Flanders. He was a member because he wanted to represent the people and to defend the rights of the people! My father wasn't drafted into the army, and after WWI he was sentenced to the death penalty because he was a member of the Parliament of Flanders. However in 1919, he received a pardon for his sentence. From 1921 to 1927 he was a member of the Daensist Party or movement, then he became a member of the Frontbeweging or Front Movement, and finally the Flemish Nationalist Party. Sadly my father passed away due to organ failure in 1933; he was only 53 years old. Because there were no successors to take over his company, the family was forced to sell. These were difficult times for our mother (born 1882). My two brothers were both students in architecture, and both became professors at the University of Ghent. I went to school in Ghent, and I finished high school there in 1939. At the University of Ghent, I followed my interest in veterinary medicine as I wanted become a veterinarian. My time as a student was cut short because the university was forced to close in May 1940 because of the war in the West. I found a job as an accountant at the German airbase in Ghent, and still today I'm getting a little pension for that!

Becoming a Volunteer

In 1941, the Flemish Labor Service or Arbeitsdienst für Flandern was founded to which I reported as a volunteer. I received my basic training in Antwerp, and immediately after, I was placed in an office with the staff. I had to take care of the recruiting department. Just after the outbreak of Barbarossa in July 1941, the "Flemish Legion" was established to recruit more soldiers for the Wehrmacht. A lot of young men – just like me – saw an opportunity to go and fight against Bolshevism. Now you have to understand that even before Barbarossa, the priests in the church were already preaching and asking the members of the church if they wanted to be under the rule of Rome or Moscow. That was an easy question of course, and with the first opportunity that arose, I volunteered for the Legion. On August 6, 1941, I arrived in the training camp or Truppenübungsplatz in Debica near Krakow. A lot of my comrades became very sick after a few days in the training camp because of the dark German bread that they had to eat. One has to understand that in Flanders we only ate white bread. Soon the medical staff found out about this problem and for the rest of our stay in Debica, we were only given white bread! Training wasn't that pleasant because the Germans treated us like dirt. At the end of August, we went to the grenade launcher training camp in Arys in Eastern Prussia. We stayed there until October 31, 1941, and I can assure you that training was very hard there. Our company was the "4.Kompanie", and we had two MG and one platoon of grenade launchers. Altogether we were 250 men strong. It was during our training in Arys that we received the famous blood type tattoo on our arm. During our stay in Arys, we sang a lot of marching songs, especially the song of the Flemish Legion: "Het Vlaams Legioen Kameraad, Rukt op ten bevrijdende daad..." (The Flemish Legion comrade, thrusts towards a liberating act...)

The Leningrad Front

On November 1, 1941, we were transferred to the front just south of Leningrad. Since winter had started early that year in Russia – mid-October to be more precise – we found a thick layer of snow upon our arrival with temperatures of -20 and even colder. At first we were accommodated in the homes of some local families. They were simple but very friendly people who took really good care of us. Sadly enough, most of their homes were destroyed by the Russian

Schwerer Granatwerfer Zug - 4.Kp/I. Btl/67. Rgt/III. SS-Panzer Korps

artillery barrages, so we had to relocate. This forced us to stay outside in the cold. We used our empty grenade and ammunition boxes to build some sort of shelter, but it wasn't that easy as the ground was frozen solid. Our uniforms were not the typical winter uniforms many people think we had; we didn't even had a "Wintermantel" ("winter jacket"). It was so cold, and we were freezing day in day out. Because of that, every day we were looking forward to get a warm meal and some hot coffee, just to warm up a little bit. Another thing we did to stay warm is to take the warm winter boots from dead Russian soldiers. Lots of us had frozen hands and feet which incapacitated us for a while. There was nothing you could do, as half of your body was frozen. My hands and feet were frozen during the winter of 1942 and 1943, which resulted in all the nerves in those body parts damaged.

Waffen-SS in action on the Russian front with a heavy mortar.

Germania's Assault Generation

We were equipped with the heavy grenade launcher 34, or Granatwerfer 34, which is an 80 mm. It was a small and lightweight grenade launcher or mortar. It was easy to carry, and it was usually operated by a crew of three: the Geschützführer, the Richtschützen, and the Ladeschützen. Each and every one of them carried a piece of the grenade launcher: the bottom plate and frame were carried on the back with a special harness, and the barrel was carried over the shoulder. Then there were about six men that carried the ammunition boxes. The barrel was about 1 meter long, and a well-trained crew could fire off thirteen grenades per minute! Obviously there had to be enough ammunition. Three "Gruppen" or section of nine men for each section formed a Zug or platoon.

Because of the extremely fast advance of the German Army and the extreme temperatures during my first winter at the front, we had to deal with a lot of problems. Because of the heavy snowfall, we had to put snowshoes on which came in handy as we were able to advance faster through thick snow. On January 27, 1942, I was wounded for the first time. Thank God I was wearing my helmet, otherwise I would've been killed for sure! A piece of shrapnel from an exploding grenade hit my helmet and got embedded into my skull. A couple of my comrades carried me to the rear of the front line, and from there I was transported to the field hospital in Krasnowadeisk. I was transported from there to the hospital in Riga where the doctors had to remove my helmet. After my recovery, I traveled over Königsberg to Göttingen for rehabilitation. Because of the cold, my hands and feet had been frozen and I developed a bladder problem (my bladder became very weak), which was uncomfortable and painful at the same time.

In May 1942, I ended up in Graz in the new "Adolf Hitler Kaserne", where I joined the Genesungs-Kompanie. There was a female RAD camp nearby which we visited frequently during our stay

Schwerer Granatwerfer Zug - 4.Kp/I. Btl/67. Rgt/III. SS-Panzer Korps

in Graz. The ladies there were very open and friendly, and we often went dancing with them (which was actually forbidden during the war), or we took them out for coffee. For some reason, the Flemings always had a lot of success with the ladies, but don't ask me why. I was having a good time there in Graz, and I fondly think back on my time there. In Graz, one was able to get his operator license, ranging from a simple motorbike to a big Panzer! We were completely surprised by that and we had a fantastic time there when obtaining our license. We were so proud of ourselves after we passed the course. I was very happy with my motorcycle license. On a motorbike one could cruise through the country and leave all his problems behind. Little did I know that my motorcycle license would come in handy later during the war. Sadly enough the time in Graz went by too quickly, and in July 1942, just like many others of my group, I had to return to the Eastern Front. This time I ended up in the swamps at the Wolchow Front.

The Wolchow

The Wolchow swamps were a horrible place. Across the swamp there were many wooden pathways, but if one would divert from one of them, usually he ended up dead. One could easily drown in the swamps. But the swamps were not the only danger. The partisans were also very active in this area! Many times we were shot at from behind as these guys were hiding in the trees. It was here in the Wolchow that General Andrey Vlassov was captured. He was the one that later fought on our side against the Russians. Another problem in the swamps were the billions of mosquitoes! They made our life a real hell. Many of us started smoking because it would keep these damn beasts away! Every day we were given three cigarettes which was not very generous. Luckily I had an uncle who had a cigarette factory. Every month he would send me a full carton of cigarettes which I obviously shared with my comrades. This made me very popular at that time.

I was wounded for the second time on August 9, 1942. A bullet went straight through my elbow but luckily it was only a flesh wound. However because of my wound, I had to go to the field hospital in Elbing which was located at the Ostsee or Baltic Sea. I spent several weeks in Elbing, followed by one week of vacation to my hometown Ghent. It was a fantastic feeling to see all my family and friends back after spending more than a year at the front. In October 1942, I was sent back to the front, this time to Alexandrowka. There we spent the night in local homes and in a military camp. Around Alexandrowka, the battles were very brutal. From the trenches, we had to fight the Russians, and every day we had to send out recon patrols. Obviously these men were all volunteers for the job, but many of them didn't come back. Sarcastically we called it the Himmelfahrtskommando, or suicide squad. But the camaraderie was so good that one would just take the risk to go on a recon patrol. Sometimes twenty to fifty men volunteered at the same time, sometimes an entire platoon! Most of the time however, none of them came back. Another squad was then sent to the rescue and to observe the situation, however we never knew what happened to our comrades that had disappeared. Just the fact of not knowing what had happened to them was very hard for us. We knew that the Russian were very brutal towards German soldiers, we've seen lots of evidence of that at the front, so we were genuinely afraid that our comrades would've fallen into enemy hands. In the meantime, we were constantly under attack by Russian tanks to which our 80 mm grenades were no match at all. Every now and then a Stuka would bravely attack these Russian tanks.

Schwerer Granatwerfer Zug - 4.Kp/I. Btl/67. Rgt/III. SS-Panzer Korps

The Crazy Russians

In the trenches, we also had to fight the crazy Russian infantry. Man to man fighting was a common thing at the Eastern Front, and our bayonets were used almost on a daily basis. We were surprised at how the Russians would storm towards our positions...running into their deaths. At that point in time, I realized that for the Russians, a human life was worth nothing. The first line had rifles while the second through fourth line only had ammunition. When a man in the front row would fall, another man from the second row would pick up the rifle and continue fighting until he would fall, and then the man in the third row would pick up the rifle, etc. The Russians suffered an enormous amount of casualties because of this tactic. We were always told to take care of the wounded and the dead. We would never leave them on the battlefield, but the Russians were different. They would leave all the bodies in the field. This went on until March 1943. Here I also suffered my first case of snow blindness; the second time was in 1944. This took me out of combat for two weeks. With bandages over my eyes, I was sent to the rear where I just had to sit and wait. Not being able to see was terrible! In the meantime, we were equipped with the new Granatwerfer 42 which was a 120 mm instead of 80 mm. This weapon increased our firepower significantly. The downside was that this grenade launcher was a lot larger and heavier. The barrel was almost 2 meters long, and a crew was only able to launch 8 grenades per minute instead of 13. The crew for a Granatwerfer was four instead of three, and it had to be transported on a carriage.

In June 1943, I contracted jaundice and ended up in Bad Tölz. Just before that, I was awarded the Nahkampfspange or close combat clasp in bronze. I subsequently went to Beneschau to the Truppenübungsplatz Milowitsch where our battalion received extra manpower due to the heavy losses suffered on the Eastern Front. In

Germania's Assault Generation

Milowitsch, we trained the new recruits, but the locals were not friendly towards us. They avoided us at all costs. On January 1, 1944, we were sent back to the Eastern Front, this time to Shitomir in the Ukraine. Once we arrived in Shitomir, we had to start our retreat immediately: forty kilometers per day with full equipment! Retreat was something that we never experienced before, so it was a bitter pill for us to swallow. We experienced ammunition shortages, and now and then there was not enough food. The situation became worse every day. In the meantime, a Panzer IV from the Das Reich Division was accidentally shot and destroyed by friendly fire. During the day, we were always fighting, and by night we were on the road again to our next position.

In March 1944, I was wounded for the third time during a dramatic trench fight. During a man to man fight, I was hit by a rifle butt on the right side of my face. You can still see the mark on my face to this day! After he hit me in the face, he turned his rifle and wanted to stab me with the bayonet. Thank God I was able to grab his rifle, turn it, and ram it into his body. If I hadn't done this, I wouldn't have survived the war. Russian bayonets were sharpened on both sides of the blade which made them very dangerous. After I killed this Russian, there was no time to sit and reflect about what happened. There was no time to grieve, as the fight had to continue. During the war we had no choice; it was either him or me. Lots of my comrades had difficulties when they just killed an enemy soldier Most of them had to throw up or they had to take a break for a few days. Some of us just kept on fighting. I was brought to the rear by a couple of comrades, and once again ended up in a field hospital. I went through a couple more field hospital visits, but every time they were moved more and more to the rear.

At the end of the retreat, I ended up in Jampol in the Ukraine. There we were surrounded, but we had to find a way to break

Schwerer Granatwerfer Zug - 4.Kp/I. Btl/67. Rgt/III. SS-Panzer Korps

through, otherwise we would be captured by the Russians, and of course that was not an option! All of a sudden we got the order to break out, and we did. We lost a lot of men during this desperate action, and I saw them falling like mosquitoes. It was horrible, but we were able to escape to "freedom" again. By the end of March 1944, I ended up in Dnjepopetrowsk, where the Russians kept on pushing us back with a tremendous force. We had no option but to retreat. In front of us there was the Dnjepr River which we had to cross. However, the river was full of ice and the water was bitterly cold. We searched for some tree trunks to help us to cross the river. We put the tree trunks in the water, and while holding on to them, we crossed the river. Many comrades were too weak and slipped off. They disappeared forever in the ice cold water of the Dnjepr River. When we reached the other side of the river, we had to march for several hours in our soaked uniforms until we reached our lines. There we were put into trucks and we drove through Romania, through the Carpathians, towards Hungary. There we were accommodated in local farms where we found lots of wine in their wine cellars. We sure did like their wine! The next day we were able to clean up and wash ourselves. Apparently the smell that emanated from us was so horrible that the farmers offered to wash our uniforms. The locals were very friendly to us, and we were very grateful for what they did for us.

The Narva Front

The restructuring of our unit happened in Beneschau in the Czech Republic. Here the 67.Rgt. was refreshed with new troops. In June, we reached a strength of 1200 men, and immediately we were put onto a transport to Narva. It was in Narva that we fought a major battle until the end of September 1944. When we arrived just west of Narva on July 15, I could tell that our troops there were already anxiously waiting for us. They were happy with the reinforcements as the Russians aggressively attacked our positions with infantry, artillery, and tanks. Their objective was to cut off a part of the German troops in order to isolate them. There at the "Blue Mountains", one of the small mountains received a special name from us, we met with our comrades from Denmark, Finland, and Estonia. We were ordered to occupy the "Kinderheimhöhe" from which we would have a good view of the Russian positions. Since July 26, after only one week of heavy fighting, we had lost most of our officers. They were all killed by a grenade impact while they were inside a bunker. The new "Tannenberg" defense line ran from Narva over the Kinderheimhöhe, the Grenadierhöhe, and the Liebeshöhe to the Gulf of Finland. Every hill was occupied by German troops. On our left we had our Dutch comrades with "De Ruyter." The Russian artillery shelled our positions continuously that day, so we were not able to move our positions. A Russian infantry attack on our positions was imminent. But from the Gulf of Finland we received support from our battleships that were present there. They opened fire on the Russian positions, hitting them with such precision that it was almost surreal. However our ships didn't have enough ammunition, so the bombing wasn't enough stop the Russians. All of a sudden we heard the Russian infantry scream "Hurrah!", and we knew they were coming. Because there were too many of them, we had to retreat together with our Danish comrades. During our retreat, we got our courage back, and we decided to counter-attack with our (machine) pistols, bayonets, and spades. It was a hard man to man battle, and all around us we could hear injured soldiers scream from pain. But there was no time to take care of the wounded and the dead, which hurt us a lot. Who knows what the Russians did with the injured and dead? That day the Kinderheimhöhe changed owners three times! And this went on for eleven days, back and forth, back and forth. Because there was no time to dig trenches, we had to dig foxholes to have a little bit of protection against the Russians projectiles. Sometimes the Russian tanks would drive over the foxhole when the soldier was still in there. The tank would stop with its tracks on top of the foxhole and then started turning, killing the soldier who was in there. It was horrible to witness such cruelty, but there was nothing we could do as we didn't have any anti-tank weapons. During this battle, one of our men became a real hero. He was an SS-Sturmmann and Richtschütze of a 7.5 PAK 40 of our 3rd Company, and his name was Remi Schrijnen (born in 1921, and wounded 8 times during the war). His courage and determination wouldn't be surpassed by many others. Even during an enormous tank attack, he maintained his calm and shot one tank after the other; sometimes 7 in one day! For his heroic actions, he was awarded the Knight's Cross of the Iron Cross on September 21, 1944. He was even mentioned in the Wehrmachtsbericht. He was true hero and example for all of us! Remi passed away in 2006. I will never forget this courageous "small fella" with his friendly sparkly eyes.

Waffen-SS troops at the Narva front in 1944.

Germania's Assault Generation

On August 6, we couldn't hold our positions against the Russians, and we had to retreat. We had only one officer left in the entire battalion! At the Grenadierhöhe, we had our last meeting place from where we fired all our grenades at the attacking Russians. Later they called our hill the fire-spitting hill. With the next Russian tank attack, we received some unexpected help from 12 Panther tanks which reduced the Russian tanks to a pile of rubble. These Panther tanks were phenomenal. At that moment, Schrijnen's PAK got hit, but he managed to survive. Since the last PAK had no more ammunition left, their crews had to retreat as well. In this sector only 2 km, wide there were 113 Russian tanks against 12 Panther tanks, two PAK, and a few grenade launchers with a total of 50 men. And because all the German officers were killed in action, it was the first time that our company was under the command of a Flemish officer! After the Battle of Narva, Leon Degrelle came to congratulate his men of the Walloon Division. This is the point where a physical fight ensued between us and the Walloons. They called us, as usual, "les salles Flamands", or the dirty Flemings. We were so fed up with them that we physically attacked them. Degrelle tried to break up the fight but he received a good beating as well. We won the fight against the Walloons that day! And this is something that people don't know, but we never got along with the Walloons!

The fighting in Narva was most likely one of the bloodiest fights ever fought during WWII, and I can attest to that! It was in Narva that I was awarded the Wound Badge in Silver, and the Iron Cross First Class. It was during the morning parade that some fellow soldiers and I received our awards. I received my Iron Cross First Class for my actions as a Granatwerferführer. Remi received his Knight's Cross, and several others were awarded the German Cross in Gold. We were given these awards personally by SS-Obergruppenführer und Kdr. des III. Gemanischen SS-Panzerkorps

Schwerer Granatwerfer Zug - 4.Kp/I. Btl/67. Rgt/III. SS-Panzer Korps

Felix Steiner! Since there weren't enough awards, he took his own from his uniform and handed them out to us. That was a gesture we would never forget. From Narva we went to Tallinn/Reval. There we were put on the "Gotland", which was a ship that had to bring us to Swinemünde. The ship was overcrowded because all the troops had to leave as soon as possible. The moment we left the harbor, we were afraid of being hit by a Russian submarine. There was still potential danger while being at sea. From the once 1200 men, only 37 soldiers and 1 officer survived the Battle of Narva! All others were killed in action or wounded which was complete madness. We arrived three weeks later in the Truppenübungsplatz Hammerstein in Pomerania. We were completely burnt out! We stayed with the local farmers and we helped them with some work here and there in the field. This was our vacation since we were unable to go back to our Fatherland, as the Americans were already there.

After the restructuring of our unit, we ended up in the Lüneburger Heide where we stayed with the locals. It was there that on October 28, 1944 the 27.Freiwilligen-SS-Grenadier-Division Langemarck was born whilst we were only at the strength of a brigade. Mid-December we were moved to the area around Köln or Cologne where we were kept as a reserve for the upcoming offensive in the Ardennes. If we were actually deployed for this offensive, then we most likely had to invade Flanders. But they didn't use us, and we were moved back to the Lüneburger Heide. We were moved to Arnswalde at the beginning of January 1945. Here we had to defend a bridgehead, but we were not able to hold it as the Russian forces were just too superior to ours. In the recaptured areas, I witnessed what the Russians had done to the locals: they nailed kids and women to barn doors, the men's eyes had been poked out and their genitals cut off, and some of them were drowned in the sceptic tanks. We were perplexed and shocked from the brutality these Russians soldiers had shown the locals, and for this we hated them even more now! But these brutalities, these crimes, were never brought up at the end of the war. None of them were prosecuted for war crimes after the war, which is a total disgrace.

The Last Months of the War

In March 1945, I was awarded the Panzervernichtungsabzeichen or the tank destruction badge. One day we were marching along a way when all of a sudden T-34 tanks loomed up on the horizon. The tanks were coming our way, so we had to take cover as soon as possible. The tanks came closer and we were genuinely scared; we had no ammunition or weapons to fight them. The tanks stopped right next to where we were hiding and funny enough, I asked one of my comrades if one of them still had a Haftmine or a limpet mine (magnetic mine). And guess what? One of them still had one! I took it from him and ran to the first T-34. I got on the tank, and I attached the Haftmine onto the turret. Thank God that thing stayed in placed and didn't come off. I jumped off the tank and took cover. Then a big explosion happened, you'd feel the shockwave, and the turret was blown off the hull of the tank. You could also hear the dreadful crying of the soldiers who were still inside the hull of the tank. Poor guys. Even today I can still hear them crying. It was horrible but I had no choice. Unfortunately this is how it goes in battle...this is war, and war is brutal and pointless. Because I blew up this Russian tank, and because of fear for revenge from the Russians, we made sure to clear the area and run away as fast as we could.

At Zachan, Stargard, Stettin, and Brüsow we fought our way back to Prenzlau, just east of Berlin. There we had no more contact with the enemy, and we were given civilian clothes. From there we were free to go: or go home or try to get to the British in the Lüneburger Heide. We didn't want to get captured by the Russians because we

Schwerer Granatwerfer Zug - 4.Kp/I. Btl/67. Rgt/III. SS-Panzer Korps

heard that they would just shoot their POWs. I always kept one bullet in my pistol which I was planning to use on myself if I were captured by the Russians. However I was able to travel to Liege in Belgium. From there I wanted to take the train to Brussels and travel to Spain because it was still under the rule of Franco. I also knew a lot of members of the Blue Division, so I could easily stay with one of them. But on my way to Spain, I was arrested in the train station in Brussels. This was the end of my flight. I was beaten with sticks because I was a former member of the SS. I was beaten unconscious, and I was dropped off at the prison in Brussels. Most of the members of the SS had their blood type tattoo on their arm. It was a typical mark which was known by enemy troops, so many of us tried to remove it before being capture by burning it, or cutting it out of the skin. I tried to bite it out of my skin but I was unsuccessful. Today I'm still proud of my blood type tattoo which is the letter "O".

After spending a couple of weeks in Brussels, we were all transported to Ghent. There we were put in a factory with all the other German POWs and collaborators. There we were awaiting trial, and almost all of us were sentenced to death! And so was I...twice! Once in June and once in September 1945. After sentencing, we were brought back to prison where they treated us very badly and where the food was horrible. Frequently we were beaten up by the guards, even if we were compatriots. In September 1945, I was brought to KZ Beverloo near Leopoldsburg in Belgian Limburg. There I stayed until the summer of 1946, waiting to be hanged. Then I was transported to the labor camp of Ruyslege where I had to work on the local farms under the supervision of the camp guards. I was set free on January 19, 1950, but that was because my mother had paid a bribe to get me out. How she managed to pay the bribe I don't know because all our family assets were taken by the government in 1944...even all of our bank accounts were seized! I went to my mother in Ghent where she was living in a small house. It was strange to get into a small house, as we used to live in a big villa before the war. The "aftershock" of the war still continued for me in the form that I had to report myself weekly at the local police station. I was also forbidden to work, so I didn't really have a future in Belgium. The only thing that kept my morale up was that I was able to marry my sweetheart in my hometown of Ghent on January 24, 1951 (which is also my birthday!). Because I had no future in Belgium, I finally made the decision in May 1954 to flee to Germany with my wife and kids. I arrived in Lövenich in the Cologne area where my brother-in-law was a branch manager with SAG (an electricity company with 7000 employees at that time).

Before I end, I want to tell you something about the weapons that we had at the front besides our Granatwerfer. As a Granatwerfer Zug we were equipped with Italian MPs, and we were using Italian ammunition. We had no K98 because they were too long and we couldn't carry a long rifle when we were carrying the grenade launcher on our back. After the Leningrad Front, I received the MP38 and a sidearm, but I was never issued the StG 44. The StG 44 was too long as well to carry with the grenade launcher. About my medals: I kept them all! The souvenir hunters were not able to take them from me, so all the medals that are in my home are the ones that I received during the war. When I was captured I hid all my medals in one of my socks and they never found them!

I've never forgotten my old comrades and my homeland. For many years I was a guest of HIAG Reutlingen and I attended many of the meetings. These were unforgettable moments in my life. Many people see us as traitors, but my question to them is simple: "What did I betray?" I never betrayed Belgium because I'm not a Belgian, I'm a Fleming! I was a soldier and I'm proud of what I have done. If I could do it again knowing what had happened back then, I'd say no.

Schwerer Granatwerfer Zug - 4.Kp/I. Btl/67. Rgt/III. SS-Panzer Korps

I have absolutely no regrets. My hope is that the generations of today and tomorrow won't see us as the monsters like so many history books like to portray the Waffen SS soldiers. I can attest that my comrades and I were honorable soldiers. To end my story, I'd like to say that war is not an option, and I sincerely hope it won't happen again. The only thing is that back then, we had no choice...

Waffen-SS soldier placing a Haftmine on a T-34.

A War Volunteer with the Hitlerjugend Division

At the beginning of 1944, I got my Wehrpass with several other "Syltters" after the military tests in Schleswig. At the beginning of December 1944, a convocation came to the RAL (Reichsausbildungslager). We were three Westerländer: Harald Koopmann, Harald Voigt and me. We should report on December 8, 1944 at 0900h in Hamburg-Altona. There was no one to help us there, however. After hours of searching, we found other future comrades who knew about it.

On December 9, 1944, we were on the way to Dresden, and from there on to Bernsdorf/Oberlausitz. Toward midnight we arrived there. We were also picked up by no one. We were very tired, however we went on our way through the empty streets as we had to find this camp. We spoke to an officer whom we met and asked for the RAL. He was not aware of the RAL in this area, but outside of town in the forest would be a Hitlerjugend Lager, and we would be expected to report there at the camp. We arrived at this camp around 0230h.

When we arrived at the camp, there was no reception at all. We had to draw attention to the windows by knocking on them. The guard came out and took us to the barracks. We were shown to our rooms, but the rooms had neither beds nor blankets. And it was super cold in there! Fortunately I had a stove in my room so I could warm up. Then an NCO who had those typical NCO braids on the shoulder showed up. He gave us a handful of wood. We tried to talk to him but he didn't listen at all. He came into the room and made a fire in the stove. Not that long later we learned that we had landed in an OT camp; OT stands for Organization Todt. The OT also built fortifications, etc. Here a workshop for tanks had to be built. In the morning when we came in, we were told that they were glad that we were finally there because they had been waiting for a long time for the Hitlerjugend to arrive. We were supposed to build the workshop as soon as possible, and we were given trowels to start with the work. We were absolutely not up for this, and we weren't even trained for this, so there must have been an error. Clearly they were expecting other people to arrive, but they had mistaken us for them. After a few phone calls, everything was sorted out, and we were allowed to leave. We were put on a train to Breslau. Around midnight, we arrived in Breslau; we were a group of youngster of 15 to 16 years old.

To Moravia

From Breslau we had to travel to Weisskirchen in Moravia first thing in the morning, meaning 0400h. Before we left Breslau, we were put in a local apartment so we could get some rest. However we got strict orders not to go into the abandoned houses in the city. Breslau was probably already quite abandoned by the population. Everything was dark and weird. I was still with some comrades in an abandoned apartment. Obviously we were all very curious and we looked around in the apartment. The apartment had been abandoned as if the residents had just gone shopping. The beds were freshly made and everything was very clean, and I remember that on the kitchen cabinet there was a big alarm clock.

The next day, it may have been around noon, we arrived in Weisskirchen, but no one was there to pick us up and bring us to the camp. It would certainly have been a good idea if we all had gone home. After a while, a car with a civilian came by, and he informed us that the camp had not yet been set up. We therefore were brought to Ollmütz for a little while. Once we got there we were accommodated in a school. At the school there were no beds or any other accommodations, and we had to wait a long time before we got something to eat. Since we had no beds we had no choice but to camp on the ground. Because our camp was not yet organized, we received some great news: for the Christmas holidays - for the first time ever – we were sent home. However I do not recall much of that Christmas in 1944. On December 28, 1944 we had to go back to Weisskirchen.

After we reported for duty, we were instructed in the house "Puschner". In our room were Harald Koopmann, W. Barg, HH, Koberg, Jung, a Pinneberger, and me. Harald Voigt, who was previously with us, was given permission to stay at home, as he was ordered to go to work with the RAD. I guess he was the only lucky one from our group because we were still expecting something to happen soon. Our platoon leader was Uffz Stössel. Our room captain was Harald Koopmann. Cleaning the rooms was our first official duty. Weisskirchen is a pretty place with several nice buildings. Bad Teplitz with its pretty hotels belonged to it. At last a certain regularity came into our existence. It began with powerful military training. But we already had some experience, so it was not really new to us. We focused a lot on terrain training, the use of the Panzerfaust, the MG42, etc. We were also trained in reconnaissance patrol. As they stated, we were made perfect and ready for combat!

On January 18, 1945, we were moved to camp 7 in Luhacowitz. The training was even more thorough there. Exercising in the snow with our winter clothes was no pleasure at all. Also the front was already coming closer and at times it sounded like an approaching thunderstorm. On the streets there were many Panzersperren and trenches built by the OT for our defense. We were asked to stay on alert for the entire time, and if necessary, we were to be equipped with weapons. Just think that at that point in time we were still the regular Hitlerjugend and not professional soldiers.

A War Volunteer with the Hitlerjugend Division

The enthusiasm was still very great among us. Each one of us would have walked blindly into battle; that's how ready we were to defend our Fatherland. The propaganda school, the training camp, etc had done a good job of indoctrinating us. We only obeyed orders; we had to obey orders, as we had no other choice. Obviously we thought it was all right. It actually went so far that we even thought when the Russians would show up that we would push them back to the Volga!

The young Czechs were absolutely distant from us, as they didn't want to fraternize with us at all. We would have liked to flirt with the pretty girls, there but they were ice cold to us. Not even the ten or twelve-year-old daughter of our housekeeper granted us a look.

The Waffen SS

On March 8, 1945, our training was finally over and we were told to return home. That was, obviously, a great feeling knowing that we were going back home. Bannführer Moritzen received the message of the completion of our training, however. 1400 Hitlerjugend members were ready and fully trained! Then Moritzen said: "The Führer has already summoned you to arms!" Next thing we knew is that we would be handed over to the Waffen SS. During his speech, Moritzen spoke of Germany being in the greatest danger. We were then divided into different groups: 200 men to Vienna, 50 men to the Panzer Brigade in Berlin, and the rest to the military training place in Beneschau near Prague. After this news, of course, there were long faces, and probably some tears. As far as I can remember, all had already a military passport for the army, the navy, or the Luftwaffe, but the Waffen SS had literally absorbed us into their ranks. We were then loaded onto wagons in the direction of Kienstlag. When we got off in Kienstlag, we saw nothing but Waffen SS uniforms. Already at the station we were divided into companies. Harald Koopmann and I stayed in a company. Then we went to our quarters at the local town, but most of the place looked cruelly desolate. All people were gone. And as cream on the cake, we were caught in a snowstorm as well. We were in the village of Networschitz in a small valley. In the former leather factory, a kitchen was installed for the residing troops. There was also a theater there which was constantly overcrowded with soldiers. My platoon was put in the former school. There were double beds arranged in all the classes for us. Harald Koopmann was in another platoon, so he was not posted in the school. In my platoon there were people from all parts of Germany. The next morning we were given our rifles and we received our blood type tattoo under the arm. The tattoo didn't take that long and it wasn't painful at all. Every time we had to exercise, we were still dressed in our Hitlerjugend uniforms, and not in Waffen SS uniforms. The training there was hard and ruthless.

On March 12, 1945, the entire regiment had to take the oath of loyalty to the Führer. The commander gave a speech and informed us that soon we would be deployed at the front. Our regiment called itself "Kampfgruppe Konopacki" or "Bohemia - SS Division Hitlerjugend." They also took away our current Wehrpasses in which they put the stamp of the Waffen SS inside together with a new page which had our name and unit on it. Our training went on even further. I can remember exactly the Panzerjäger training. We were to jump with a Haftmine on a moving tank and fix the mine on the turret of the tank. This was not as easy as it sounds because you did not want to get caught under the tracks!

On March 30, 1945, there was an exercise for which we were on the road for two days. We shot solid cartridges this time. It all happened in a beautiful area. But for such an exercise, there wasn't too much time, as ammunition was getting scarce and the front was coming closer. We returned to our quarters after this exercise. In the evening the place was set on high alert, and no one was allowed to leave the village this time. At any moment the order could come to move out, and we were all given live ammunition.

Young Waffen-SS soldiers – location unknown.

Moving to the Front

On April 5, 1945, at 1600h the order was given to move out. We were provided with extra food, and we received weapons of all kinds and first aid kits. Our trainers remained our superiors, and some of them were highly decorated, for example with the Knight's Cross. We were loaded on trucks and we drove towards the front. The trip went through Bohemia, Niederdonau, via Znojim, to Krems. On April 7, 1945, in the evening at Krems am Donau, we were placed on the front line. We had to dig ourselves in and stay under cover while "guarding" the Danube. The view across the Danube was delightful. The Russian should be over there, but I haven't seen a single one of them yet. There were no shots fired, and everything remained quiet. Next to our positions lay a unit of former Flak soldiers; these were for the most part elderly people. When they saw us they shook their heads and said: "Guys, just go home." We were strictly forbidden to speak to them!

The next day we were withdrawn from our positions, but at nightfall we had to go back. This became our routine for the next couple of days. We didn't fire a single shot and everything remained quiet at the front. On April 16, 1945, we were moved to the village south-east of Lanthaya. There we had to dig in again as a second line of defense. Our platoon leader ordered my comrade and I to carry a seriously wounded soldier from another unit back behind our lines. We had to carry him on an improvised stretcher which was made of a piece rug. The wounded soldier had sustained some serious injuries: I could clearly see that the skin of his belly area was blown away, and I could see his intestines. He was still alive, but he was in a twilight zone: at some moments he was unconscious, and then he was awake again. While we were carrying the wounded soldier, we were completely exposed to enemy fire however they never fired one single shot at us. However on our way back to the front line, we were shelled with grenades. We made it back to our positions and we were happy to have survived our first firefight.

We were repositioned again, and we were moved to a different location. With two groups, we were on the left of a road leading to a small village. My group was lying in a hollow path, and we were protected by natural wall about 2 meters high. To the right of us, about 15 to 20 meters further, where the other group was located lay, the path had no protection at all. The following night a tragedy took place, for a Russian SMG (heavy machine gun) had positioned itself at about 30 meters away from us. This SMG killed almost the entire group, together with the group leader, during the night. Exactly how it happened I don't know, as everything was so dark at night and you couldn't see a thing. Our group was safe and out of range of the

A War Volunteer with the Hitlerjugend Division

SMG fire. The SMG fire kept going until dawn. Then it was all quiet again. We had to take care of the wounded comrades who had been lying to the right of us, but only a few had survived. They had been laying there during the entire night bleeding out, and there was nothing we could do until the SMG stopped firing at us. It was horrible!

On the other side of the road, behind a hill, not visible from the village, lay the rest of our company. They told us that we should join the rest of the company as soon as possible. We had to cross a street which exposed us to the Russian positions in the village. Every now and then we were able to get some cover by the hedges which were growing on the side of the street. All of our group made it safely to the rest of the company; none of us was hit by enemy fire! I was the last man to come in and on my way to the rest of the company I observed a Russian MG nest about halfway between the village and our positions. Fortunately for me, the Russians were all dead. Now that we had all regrouped, we were about to attack the village. These are the moments that one will never forget. These minutes before an attack seemed to last for hours. The waiting was annoying and nerve wracking. To take the village was not as difficult as expected, however we had a lot of trouble with our rifle ammunition. They were lacquer-coated iron cartridges which remained stuck for a short moment in the gun barrel after firing a shot. This was not exactly reassuring while in the midst of a combat scene. Once we arrived in the village, we searched all the houses, barns, etc. On the street lay a dead Russian officer with a split skull. I took his pistol, but one of our officers came up to me and asked me to hand over the pistol. There had been a lot of looting in the houses, and a Russian was caught by another platoon during a house search. Apparently he had mistreated a woman, and for this he was shot right away.

Germania's Assault Generation

I almost shot a German woman, when from behind a closed cellar door, I saw someone aiming at me through a hole in the door. Without hesitating I fired a shot, but thank God I missed. The woman just tried to make herself visible to us by sticking a piece of pipe out of the door. I approached her, and she told me that the Russians had taken some of the women from the village. But whatever horrible things that had happened in the village, we were not given much time to reflect on it. Actually there was no time to reflect on things at all, and soon we withdrew from the village.

The Russians had not been stopped, and they were coming closer and closer. There seemed to be an endless supply of Russian soldiers, while our unit was getting smaller and smaller. Every time we moved our positions, we did a head count. One time one of my friends was missing. It was strange because he was in the foxhole not far from mine. After re-grouping, our platoon leader said we had failed to safely maintain our positions, and that the distances between foxholes was too big. Because of that, I was ordered to go back and search for my missing friend. Maybe he was just sleeping in another foxhole? I went back alone, not knowing if the Russians were already there! It was half-dark when I arrived, and discovered that my friend was dead. I stayed there until the early morning, and when it was light I noticed that his rifle was red from his blood.

Another experience I surely do remember is that one of our group leaders (a Fahnenjunker) talked with our platoon leader (they were friends with each other). The platoon leader was highly decorated, and he handed over a letter to the Junker and said, "I do not think I'll get out of here alive, so if I fall on the field of honor, then please give this letter to my fiancée." Instead the Junker was more out to get an Iron Cross First Class. Thereupon the Junker was then allowed to select some volunteers for a kind of reconnaissance mission. When he came back from his mission, most of his men were

A War Volunteer with the Hitlerjugend Division

dead and the number of Russian POWs he brought back was not impressive at all. Whether he got the Iron Cross or not I cannot say. The conversation he had with the platoon leader afterwards was certainly embarrassing to both of them. Unfortunately I do not know the names of these two officers. I forgot a lot of specific dates and places, however I was able to retrieve lots of information from my former "Kriegskamerad" Harald Koopmann from his personal diary, which he was able to bring home despite war and captivity. I am very grateful to him for that. Sure, many soldiers had similar experiences but since we were only 15 and 16 years old at the time, I always wanted to keep as much information as possible.

Sharing Foxholes

I shared a foxhole with Koopmann, and our foxhole was our home, our kitchen, our toilet, and our bedroom, and it was constantly under attack from sniper rifles and MG with explosive ammunition. One time, three grenades were specifically fired at our foxhole: one fell on the right side, one on the left, and the last one 2 meters behind it. Usually if there was a fourth one, it would directly hit the foxhole, but it never happened. We were very lucky that day, but it could be over in the blink of an eye. Death was all around back in those day.

I had once put my cookware on the edge of our foxhole. Then you'd hear a "peng", and the cookware was gone. In our line of fire, one of our men was killed in action. Rumor has it that he had been accidentally shot by his own people. He supposedly moved to the holes at night with an open coat and without a password. The Russians also advanced like this. He paid the ultimate price for his careless actions. We must have been quite filthy because washing and change of linen was not an option. In my foxhole I often dreamed of sleeping once again in a real bed. I wanted to remember the sound of the bedroom door at home.

Sharing a fox hole...

At night, we got the order that when a green light ball appeared, it meant we had to retreat. There were lots of light ball shot in the air that night, but we hadn't seen a green one. It was already day again, and there was still no command to move. The Russians stopped shooting a while ago, so we kept quiet until the evening. Then we realized that the Russians were on the left and right of our platoon's location. We were fortunate enough to have an experienced platoon leader; maybe 20 or 30 soldiers were left in our platoon. We could hear the Russians with their trucks, they were very close, but they probably thought we were all gone, otherwise it would've been the end for us. As soon as it was safe to move, we gathered around our platoon leader and we started marching. We moved through creeks and bushes, as this was a lot safer than using the regular roads. We had a lot of confidence in our platoon leader, as he seemed to know what he was doing. We also had to avoid towns, open terrain, etc. We marched without a compass or maps and somehow, to our great despair, we realized all of a sudden that we were behind the Russian lines! So we were marching in the wrong direction!

A War Volunteer with the Hitlerjugend Division

I do not know how long it took us, but we finally made it through the Russian lines. Probably the Russians had gathered on the main roads to continue their push to the west while we slipped through the little holes. If we had tried to get through the Russian lines fighting, then none of us would've survived. On our way back, we came into no man's land. The German troops had most likely already left this area. Then we came into a city that was totally deserted and dark. We went in search for some food, and we found a large supply camp of the Wehrmacht. It was guarded by a soldier (perhaps an officer) from which the eagle and shoulder pieces had already been cut off. The only catch was that man did not want to give us access to the camp. Our platoon leader said, "Guys, you go to the next corner and make sure the area is safe." While our platoon leader stayed behind at the camp entrance we went to secure the perimeter. Suddenly we heard a shot, and then there was silence. We ran back to the camp entrance, and we saw the camp guard laying on the ground: dead! Our platoon leader had shot the man, but we didn't question his action. We entered the camp, and we found lots of food. We ate everything that we could find. I was eating lard with my hands, which would cause an upset stomach or diarrhea. After our "meal", we packed all the food that we could, and shortly after that, we were on the road again. After a long march, we finally were reunited with our old unit, or what was left of it. According to the diary of Harald Koopmann, there were about 16 men. Add those 16 men to our platoon, and we were almost at full strength again. This must have been close to the end of April 1945. We found wounded soldiers all over the place, however since there were no more field hospitals available, all the wounded were lying on the ground or trying to keep up with a unit. We had a wounded comrade in our unit. He had a fractured leg, but he had it wrapped up so that he could stay with us. But the Russians were coming closer, and when we looked behind us we estimated that they were only 2 km behind us...and they were getting closer! Suddenly an officer in his staff car drove by, and we stopped him. We asked if he would be so kind to take our wounded comrade with him, but he simply refused. He gave us a bogus reason, and off he went! We had no choice to leave our comrade behind; he must have been only 16 years old. Our platoon leader gave him his pistol before we left, and that was the last time we saw him. This happened near Zneim (Zuojmo).

Retreating from the Front

But at that time there was no time left to think about these things and to become sentimental. We were in a hurry to leave as soon as possible. While we marched in columns, we were constantly overtaken by trucks and horse-drawn wagons. Because I was so exhausted, I could easily fall asleep while marching, so I asked the platoon leader if I could catch a ride with another four more men with a truck that just stopped. This was allowed under the one condition to wait for our unit in the next village. We jumped on the truck and drove to the next village where we patiently waited for the rest of the unit to arrive. Soon it started to become dark, but our unit was still not there. Where were they? The village was completely dark and deserted, so we had to set up a guard. Not a lot later, we could hear the engines of approaching tanks. Now we became really nervous as we didn't know if they were ours or not. The first tank drove by, but we were not sure if it was a German tank. When the second one loomed up, we could clearly see that they were ours. Obviously we stopped the tank, and we asked the commander if we could catch a ride with them. He happily told us to jump on the tank, and off we went. These tanks were King Tigers, and they were huge! The good thing is that it was nice and warm sitting close by the engine, and on the glowing exhaust, we were able to bake potatoes. The tank crew told us that the Russian were pushing with such a tremendous force that there was no way to fight their advance. While

A War Volunteer with the Hitlerjugend Division

riding on the tanks, I passed Harald Koopmann. I asked him to meet in the next village, but he refused. A bit later, he fell into captivity when his unit was encircled by enemy forces. In our case, we drove west while still sitting on these huge tanks. While driving though the country, we could clearly see what the Russian airplanes had done to the retreating troops and civilians. There were lots of destroyed trucks, wagons, and other equipment lying around, while dead people and animals were spread all over the place. It was horrible! The smell of burned people and animals was so heavy that even two years after the war, I could still smell it! But among this death and destruction, there were still lots of refugees forming kilometer-long columns.

Then came the time that most of the tanks ran out of fuel. The order was given to blow these tanks up so that the Russian couldn't use them against our troops. So all the men jumped on the last running tank, and we continued our drive to the next village. When we arrived in the village, we noticed that it was full of soldiers. Somehow we were able to receive marching orders! Without marching orders, chances were relatively high that you'd end up hanging on a tree if you were caught by our military police forces. On our way to the west, we had already seen these scenarios, so we were very cautious. For some reason, I ended up on a truck with several other soldiers. When moving through the country, it was desirable to be in the company of several other soldiers. Reason why was because whoever fell into Czech hands or into the hands of released concentration camp prisoners, they knew that their future wouldn't be that bright! We all knew by then that these people would release their furious rage on all the Germans that they could catch.

We arrived in a town with a pretty castle. There were a lot of high army officers present. One of them had pity on us even though we belonged to the Waffen SS. He gave us new marching orders for our future travels. In that town, there was an open barn with a long table inside. On that table, there were women dancing and urinating in champagne glasses. I had never seen anything like that before in my life. I was really shocked, but maybe that was because I was still so young and not that enlightened. We didn't stay in that village, and we moved further west after visiting the castle first, of course. After a long adventure and countless days of marching, we arrived near an American camp. It was there that we had to throw all our weapons onto a big pile. I threw mine on there as well, but I kept my 08 pistol in my bread bag with me. A very dangerous thing to do, but I was still young so I took the risk. I had lost sight of my four comrades, and the camp was big, very big! My SS runes on my uniform were removed before I went into captivity.

SS Sammellager

All members of the Waffen SS were placed into a large Sammellager (about 10,000 men) in a large meadow. Nothing to eat and no blankets. At night it was dog-cold, and our toilet was a long ditch with a tree trunk above it where you had to sit on. Going to the toilet was always a balancing act because you couldn't hold yourself anywhere. We were very weak at this stage after the war, as we were given no food or water. The only thing we had were lice. Then after a few days, we were divided into several groups. The word spread that there would be food for all of us. Try to imagine how you could divide one can of meat and one loaf of bread between 100 men. My cigarettes helped me a lot in times that I was very hungry, because I could exchange a cigarette here and there for a small piece of bread. The inhabitants of the nearby village (unfortunately I forgot the name of it) threw bread to us, and for us this was more than a gift from heaven. The bread distributed to us by the Americans was under strict supervision, and even the bread crumbs were counted! How many prisoners died there, that I do not know. I guess it must have been hard for the "Amis" to suddenly provide for so many prisoners.

A War Volunteer with the Hitlerjugend Division

But since all of the prisoners were former Waffen SS soldiers, they didn't really care. I spent several weeks in this camp.

One day an Ami came by and looked for over a thousand volunteers who were still able to march. The Ami wanted to film something. There would be special catering and cigarettes for the participants, so immediately he got his volunteers and was able to film. Then a German higher officer commanded me to rake the ground in front of an American barrack. But I was simply too tired, and I refused this. What followed was a powerful slap in my face from this officer. Luckily, many fellow prisoners stood up and they all took a threatening attitude toward this officer. Thank God everything went quietly because the Amis were very trigger happy with their MG, and they would definitely have used it against us.

After a good ten weeks in the first camp, we were split up into different groups, and we were put into different camps. I ended up in a former airfield. We were lodged in a former hangar; the lice were all gone by then since we went through a delousing process several times. Also the food was a bit better here. Beds were not provided, so we had to sleep on the ground. My stay in this camp was very short, and soon I was relocated to Plattlingen. There we had to sleep in tents made from our personal Zeltbahn, which we still had. This Zeltbahn was part of our old equipment, so we were allowed to keep them. When four of these Zeltbahnen were joined together, it was a tent for four people, although it was still a bit tight. But at least we had a roof over our heads, however these Zeltbahnen were not always water tight. In Plattlingen, the food was also very scarce. The ration of butter per day was as big as a sugar cube. Every day we had to march to work; the officers would lead at the head of the columns. They had the best position in the entire column because they were able to collect the discarded cigarettes of the Amis! Obviously a complaint was filed after a little while by other soldiers to the commander of the camp, because we wanted to march in the front every now and then. However nothing changed, and the officers always marched in the front.

When we were marching, an Austrian often stood next to me. He had a safety pin on him upon which he used to pin leftover cigarettes that he found here and there. While holding the safety pin, he would smoke the cigarettes until there was only 2 mm of cigarette left. This Austrian also collected empty cans of food which he took out of the garbage bins of the Americans' kitchen. He would boil water in them which changed the water into some sort of terrible broth. But his stomach was full! In this camp, we built a huge Barakkenlager. When they were finished, they became our home. In these constructions there were usually around 1000 men inside. We built ten of these blocks in total, and each block was fenced off with a barbed wire fence. These blocks were pretty big, as they were 100 meters x 100 meters. While constructing these blocks, I was part of a crew that did the flooring. It was not as exhausting as putting up the walls or working on the roof. I also assembled beds, together with the Austrian. It was a tough job because when a bed was finished, it had to be carried into the building by 4 men. Sometimes we were a bit too slow transporting the beds, to which the Amis would shoot a volley over our heads to make us move faster. Our guards were mostly of Jewish descent, and lots of them had lost some relatives in the concentration camps. I had no real conception of a concentration camp anyway, and the first pictures of the horror were shown to me while I was in the camp. I was called by two guards who sat on a bed. As I stood before them, one of them showed me a news magazine full of cruel images from a liberated concentration camp. His parents had also perished in Poland.

Well I was not there, and I had nothing to do with this cruelty! The other Ami beside him was very reserved, and he looked angry.

A War Volunteer with the Hitlerjugend Division

Suddenly he stood up and he wanted to kick me with his big boot in the face. The other Ami was just in time to stop him. After this little ordeal, I was sent back to work immediately. How easy-going one was at times is shown by another example. There was a guard who liked shooting cans and bottles. Then he asked if he could shoot a cigarette from my mouth. Being only 16 years old, I obviously agreed. He took his shot and the cigarette was gone. I think I got chocolate from him instead of cigarettes! I can assure you that this is something you only do once. Later this Ami would seek other volunteers for his little fun activities. In time, an Ami who was in charge of the battalion's car park took me under his wings. He always called me "Sneip". Every morning, after he had dropped off some other soldiers, he always said to me, "Snipe (Sneip), come on." I could not speak much English, and during our conversation another prisoner tried to translate. Later the Ami told me that he had no children, and had a large car repair shop with a gas station in America. He said I should come with him to America, but I didn't want to go to America with him. I wanted to go back home.

The camp had a wide street in the middle. To the left and right of the street were five camps of 1000 men each. The whole camp was about 800 meters long. Each camp had its own entrance to the street. The street was only open to one side, and secured by a large main gate. Every gate and every main entrance was of course heavily guarded. In the first camp to the right of the main entrance was the German camp management. I was lucky enough to have a job as a kind of messenger for the camp management. I brought orders and communications from the camp management to the various other camps. The camp gradually filled with prisoners from all corners of the American zone, and there was also a camp with many Russians prisoners. The entire camp, about 10,000 men, were all former SS members. There may have been other nationalities as well. Our camp leader's name was Caesar, and his deputy was Lieutenant Colonel Neumann. The camp leader was from noble descent. I think he was some sort of former "Freiherr" ("Baron") or something similar. He enjoyed great popularity in the camp, but on the other hand, his deputy Neumann was a sluggish type. He always wanted to know something about Caesar and the things he did. Our camp leader and his deputy were already over 50 years of age.

Time went by, and life in the camp became easier as the food and accommodation became a lot better than they were at the beginning. Cigarettes were also available, and they became our main currency. Things seemed to become a lot easier in the camp, and I was able to visit every camp by just showing my papers. I was probably the only one who was able to do that since I was known as the messenger. It even went so far that an Ami officer became very good friends with a Waffen SS officer. The Ami officer regularly picked up his German friend and gave him an American uniform which he had to put on. Together they went to town to enjoy the ladies there! I can assure you that if they were caught, they would've been executed, and I think the Ami officer was well aware of that. But seemingly he didn't care about the possible consequences. Obviously I knew about what they were doing, but I kept my mouth shut because; one I knew lots of people, and two because I didn't trust the Amis. In our camp there were also a couple of wounded soldiers. There were three young soldiers, probably around my age, who were severely wounded during battle. Two of them had their legs and arms blown off. Only their body and head was left, but they were still happy to be alive. Their comrades made all sorts of wooden things for these two to make their life easier. The third one still had his arms, but his legs were gone. I can't imagine how a person could live a life like that.

When things got too relaxed and easy going in the camp, the Amis became stricter again. It was then that they started interrogating people in the hopes of finding former concentration camp guards. But most of them had destroyed their identity papers and took on a new name by using false papers. Every now and then the Amis caught one, and he would be dealt with accordingly.

Christmas 1945

In 1945 I was still in Plattlingen, and most of us were homesick. There were many of us who hadn't seen their relatives and their home for two years or longer. Christmas was well organized in the camp, but it was very difficult to sing carols, as it would remind us of our families. It was probably around this time that we were allowed to write home for the first time. My parents had not heard from me since Christmas 1944. We were given special stationery from the Amis. Obviously the Amis censored our mail but that was ok since our relatives finally got mail from us. New Year's celebrations were not that special, as alcohol was strictly prohibited for us. Although there was one prisoner who was always able to get something special from the Amis, and on New Year's Eve he was able to score a bottle of liquor! In the middle of January 1946, we were relocated to Dachau, and word went around that we were going to another camp. We had to leave this camp, as we had to make room for civilian refugees.

Escape from the Camp

In Dachau we were placed in the former concentration camp, and there we heard the rumor that the camp was to be handed over to the Russians. When I heard that, I took my belongings under my arm and escaped from the still weakly-guarded camp. I met a Dutchman and another German who had the same intention. We only marched at night, and in the evening we tried to get something to eat from a local farmer. That worked well mostly. I was happy that I wasn't alone, otherwise I would've been very miserable. The fear of being caught in the forests by former concentration camp prisoners was something that also played in us. Then we saw some horses grazing in front of a farm and we didn't hesitate one moment to steal them. Horses made it a lot easier to travel. We rode mostly through the forests because we didn't want to be seen by the Amis. We wanted to go further west, and we were able to travel 200 km on these horses. My butt was so sore from riding that horse that I could barely walk. We came to a small village where we decided to sell the horses to a local farmer. We felt that the risk of getting caught became greater and greater. We got a smoked ham and several hundred cigarettes for the horses. I believe I had tears in my eyes when I had to say farewell to my faithful horse. After we sealed the deal with the farmer, an Ami showed up. While we were eating, the farmer had made his way through the back door, and told the Ami that there were three German soldiers in the yard. There were only a few Amis in the village, and I didn't have my gun with me. We didn't want to fight anyway, so the Amis took us to the house where we were made prisoners again. We had to sit down on the street side of the house and wait. I would've loved to go back inside the farm to have a chat with the farmer. First he took our horses, gave us food, and then betrayed us. And why? We were brought back to the prison in Dachau where the three of us got separated. We've never seen each other again.

Dismissed from Dachau Prison

We were about 1000 men who were transported from the prison in Dachau to the camp in Munster. Only one Ami escorted all of us on the train! It was actually the most beautiful train ride of my life. I will not forget the reception by the English at the camp in Munster. There was an entire group of heavily armed soldiers and several armored vehicles waiting for us. It was like a bad dream. I wondered if the Ami was smiling when he saw our faces. We were escorted into the camp and we had to put our luggage in front of us on the ground.

A War Volunteer with the Hitlerjugend Division

Then came an English officer with a stick under his arm (customary with the English military), accompanied by a German military officer in a green uniform. This German officer also had a cane under his arm. He was with some sort of organization that helped out the English in the camps. The German officer took away almost all our beautiful clothes, including my field bottles. More "green" soldiers would show up, and all were former German Army soldiers. Now they were part of the GSO (German Service Organization or "Dienstleistungsorganisation"). The Englishman had employed these GSO people as drivers, security guards, and interpreters.

Now there was only one thing left, and that was to go home as soon as possible. A large majority of the prisoners had already been able to inform their relatives that they were in the camp in Munster, and that they were going to be released. But they had it wrong, as the English announced that all healthy individuals were to be transported to England for work (mostly in the mines). It felt like the heavens were falling for us. The medical examinations began immediately, and they were performed by a German physician. Before the English made the announcement, everyone was healthy, but after the news about the "England trip", almost the entire camp started limping. During the medical examination, I saw my cousin Heinrich Nielsen (also from Sylt). He did not immediately recognize me. Heinrich was released because of his foot injury, and I was dismissed because I was not yet 18 years old. I simply can't describe the joy that I felt when I heard that I wasn't going to England. We were given plenty of food, and then the journey started. First we went to the Segeberg transit camp. Segeberg was also a transit camp for refugees, and the misery we saw there was indescribable. Not only did these people have to leave their possessions, but there were also many who were severely abused by the Russians. I will never forget the despair that I saw in the children's eyes there. We immediately gave away our rations to these poor people. We thought that we would be home soon, and that we would have plenty of food there. We made our way to Niebüll after we got all our paperwork in order. Traveling was made very difficult with all the checkpoints and traveling from Sylt to Paris today is certainly easier than in 1946 from Segeberg to Niebüll!

After thirteen months of imprisonment and four months of military service, it was of course an overwhelming feeling to see my street again, to see my house again. I still could not believe that I was finally walking through the front door of my home. These may be small things, but they can be of great importance in one's life. I had been home for about a year when one morning while I was still sleeping, my mother was cleaning the windows. She left all the windows and door open for ventilation, but my room door slammed shut because of a light breeze that went through the house. I had probably just dreamed of the war and I was in shock. It was so bad that my mother had to call a doctor. I still had the smell of burnt people and horses in my nose, and I didn't want to talk to anyone about my experiences. My rage against uniforms was so great that even the railway officers with their uniforms were a thorn in my eye. Politically, the time was also interesting. On election days, there were always colorful events from the different political parties with lots of people present. My friends and I visited almost all the events of all the parties, but we had yet to learn to deal with democracy...

From Demjansk to Breslau – 3.SS-Panzer-Division - "Totenkopf"

I was born in 1924 in Burg-Stargard near Neubrandenburg (located in West Pomerania approx. 50 km from the Polish border). I was the second oldest of 4 children. From 1930 to 1938, I went to school at the Volksschule in Burg-Stargard. My father was taking care of our family, and he worked as a farm hand while my mother was a professional dressmaker. After my time at the Volksschule, in the fall of 1938, I started to work in an arms factory. It was very normal at that time that the oldest children in a family went to work immediately after they finished their education. This was done to help to provide for the family. So this was the case for my oldest sister and I. My two younger sisters were able to learn a true profession. I was a bit sad that I had to go to work immediately after finishing school because I wanted to become a mechanic or electrician. Besides the activities with the Hitlerjugend, I had no other interest in joining other organizations and their activities they held. There was one reason why, and this is because as a kid I always wanted to wear a uniform.

In October 1940, I volunteered for service with the Waffen SS in Neubrandenburg which belonged to Wehrkreis II. When I turned 17, I received a notification from the SS-Ergänzungsstelle Ostsee (II) Stettin that I was accepted into the Waffen SS. My draft notice arrived on May 25, 1941, and I was attached to the SS-Ersatz-Bataillon "Nord" in Goslar am Harz. On June 21, 1941, I was already with my frontline unit, the 13.Kp. des SS-Totenkopf-Infanterie-Regimentes 3 in Stuhm in Western Prussia. In Goslar we received no training at all; we only slept there! In Stuhm, I spoke to one of the instructors and he asked me if I was interested in a particular position within the unit. I was placed with the radio operators (Funker).

147

Germania's Assault Generation

Marching into Russia

On June 24, we crossed the German-Soviet border, and pushed through to Dünaburg (Daugavpils). We stopped there on a hill just in front of a river with our Opel-Blitz "Funkwagen" ("radio truck"). I believe that this river was the River Duna. All of a sudden, a Soviet fighter plane flew over our position, followed by an ME-109. The German machine was in aerial combat with a Russian Rata (Polikarpow I-16; Rata means rat). Suddenly we saw a light flash on the horizon, and the ME-109 came back but the Rata didn't. We continued our push in the direction of the Stalin Line, which we reached at the beginning of July. There we were greeted by an energetic Soviet resistance, which we were able to fight back at the cost of many lives. The Stalin Line was hidden far into the countryside, and had a battery of bunkers and fortifications, hence the many casualties on our side. During this battle, our commander Theodor Eicke, was wounded when his staff car drove over a landmine. We continued our way to the north of Lake Ilmen (Novgorod). There we were again involved in severe battles with many casualties. Then we continued to Dno towards Demjansk. I think this was sometime in October 1941. This area was very swampy, and the advance almost came to a stop; only vehicles with tracks could move through the swampy areas without problem.

I also want to mention the battles around the Waldai Heights (Novgorod Oblast) while we were on our way to Demjansk. I was a Funker attached to the 13.Kp. We had a few heavy 15 cm infantry guns on the left and right flank of our positions while in front of us we had the cover of 20 mm FLAK guns. We were prepared for a major Russian counter-attack here. Suddenly, the order was given to open fire, and like a rolling thunder, our four infantry guns started spawning their deadly loads onto the Russian positions. I was sitting with my radio equipment in a foxhole while I was transmitting the

From Demjansk to Breslau –
3.SS-Panzer-Division - "Totenkopf"

coordinates to the "B-Stelle" ("B-Position") of our unit. While I was transmitting the coordinates, there was suddenly a heavy explosion. What happened? Carefully I came out of cover, head first, looking around me to see what had happened. I turned around and I noticed that one of our 15 cm guns had an exploded barrel. Clearly a misfire and the whole barrel exploded with serious consequences. The loader was hit in the abdomen by a piece of the gun port, and his intestines were hanging out of his body. He was screaming like crazy, asking the men to shoot him, but nobody reacted. None of us wanted to shoot him. A few minutes later, he passed away. This was my first war experience.

Waffen-SS 20 mm FLAK on a Sd. Kfz. 10/5.

A few days later, I switched to the B-Stelle with a comrade. I set myself into my new position and I set my radio up ready for transmissions. Suddenly I heard: "the Russians are attacking!" What came out the woods was an amazing but at the same time terrifying force of men and vehicles: hundreds, thousands of Russian infantrymen supported by T-34 tanks were coming our way! I was given the coordinates by our reconnaissance troops, which I immediately passed on to our artillery. The guns started firing without interruption. Also the 20 mm FLAK guns, who were positioned 300 meters on my right opened fire. What happened then is something that is almost impossible to describe. There were so many bodies in the field. I've never seen so many dead bodies in my entire life! The 20 mm FLAK surely did its job. This was one of the most horrific moments for me in the entire duration of the war. I will never forget the Waldai Heights.

The Kessel of Demjansk

At the beginning of February 1942, the circle around Demjansk closed, and it became the "Kessel" or pocket of Demjansk, or the drama of Demjansk. Hitler denied all equipment for a winter war because he believed that the Russians had already been defeated, and that there would be no new winter war. Hitler ordered to hold our positions until the last man; every man had to be able to hold his positions and fight the enemy with a fury that was never seen before. But on January 12, we already had temperatures of -52 Celsius, and we had no winter equipment. We only had our summer uniforms while the snow was waist high. The "Ostheer" wasn't equipped for winter war: the turrets of our tanks were frozen solid and were unable to move and the engines of every motorized vehicle suffered a great deal as well. We had to break our bread with our rifle butts, and amputations of extremities became routine. Because of the cold, the activities at the front were slim to none, so we could move around freely. If we were able to move. Sometimes the "Iwan" would fire a couple of shots in the air just to let us know they were still there. Their weapons never seemed to fail during wintertime. At a certain point, they were able to shoot one of our communication cables. Obviously the "Funker" were called, and we had to grab a new cable and look for the broken one to fix it. This was not an easy task at -50

Celsius while moving through very deep snow. Once the cable was fixed, we had to report back.

Waffen-SS troops in Demjansk.

During one of our visits to battalion HQ, we found some skis which we took with us. From now on we were not walking anymore, but rather used the skis to move from place to place. The hunger was the most difficult part of the entire experience. We were all between the age of 17 and 20, and we were all very hungry. Some of our comrades found a couple of dead horses in no man's land, and as soon they brought the news they found some meat, we armed ourselves with axes and knives and went out to grab it. With shovels, we dug the dead horses out of the snow. Some of the comrades were able to get big chunks of meat by using their axes. I strongly advised my comrades not to eat this meat since these horses had been laying there for a couple of months already. But they wouldn't listen, and the result was that five of them were transported to the field hospital. They never came back… During this time, there was only one can of meat and one loaf of bread for eight people, and this was the ration for one day. Obviously we ate everything the moment we got it, and the rest of the day we were hungry. The Kessel was provided with ammunition and food by air. The Luftwaffe dropped packages now and then on our position, but this caused them a tremendous amount of casualties. During our next visit to battalion HQ, we snatched the battalion commander's dog. We were hungry and we needed to eat something. We waited until we left the HQ, and a comrade shot the dog with his pistol. They next pulled the dog's skin over his head and they hung him up to bleed him out. The dog stayed outside for one night, and the next day we cooked the meat. We ate the dog meat without salt, and I can tell you that it was not very tasty, however we were not hungry for the next couple of hours. Besides all this misery, we were able to hold our positions. We lost many men, and I'm happy that I survived this ordeal. The severe weather conditions, our poorly equipped troops, and a strong enemy, made it sometimes very desperate for us. After our escape from the Demjansk pocket, we were moved to the rear so that we could take a little break from all the fighting. We obviously had to return to the front after a short while. This was around April or May 1942. Our engagement in the Demjansk area lasted until September 1942. Then we were sent back to Eastern Prussia for a couple of days. Like many of my comrades, I was given a leave of 4 weeks. I spent my time with my family of course. As far as I remember, all the comrades that lived to the east of Berlin and Munich were granted their "Heimaturlaub" first. When we returned to our troop, the others were sent on their "Heimaturlaub." In the meantime, the rest of our division was sent to western France to the region of Angouleme. Because of the many casualties that we suffered during the "Kessel" of Demjansk, we were given new bodies and equipment in this Occitan region. It was here where I received my new marching orders. It was in France that I completed my driving course, and that I obtained my driver's license.

From Demjansk to Breslau –
3.SS-Panzer-Division - "Totenkopf"

Like in every army, there were a lot of rumors going around, and one of them was that our division would be shipped to Africa to help Rommel out. We would be going through a new medical examination which would clear us for combat in a tropical environment. Furthermore, our blood type would be tattooed on our left upper arm. After a few days, another rumor was spread that we would be going to Russia again. We were actually very happy to hear that because there we knew our way: we were familiar with that environment. And it didn't take long before they gave us a winter uniform. We obtained the best equipment that there could be: felt boots, a medium long camo jacket with a rabbit fur liner, warm gloves, and a felt cap. Such equipment would've been a bonus during the winter of 1941/1942 which would've made life at the front a lot easier! It didn't take very long before we were shipped back to Russia in February as the SS-Totenkopf-Panzergrenadierregiment 3. From Angouleme, we traveled through Germany and Poland. After one week of traveling, we finally arrived in the Ukraine in a town called Poltawa. Upon arrival, we were immediately made ready for combat, and together with the 1.SS-Panzergrenadier-Division "Leibstandarte Adolf Hitler", the 2.SS Panzergrenadier-Division "Das Reich", and our Totenkopf Division, we became the II.SS-Panzerkorps which was under the command of SS-Obergruppenführer Paul Hausser or "Papa Hausser" as we used to call him.

Arrested by the Feldpolizei

Our objective was Charkow, and after a long battle for the city, we continued towards Donez. It was then, during a reconnaissance flight with a Fieseler "Storch," that our division commander Theodor Eicke was shot down on February 26, 1943. As a tribute to our fallen commander our SS-Totenkopf-Panzergrenadierregiment 3 received the honorary name Theodor Eicke. His name was put on the cuff title of our uniforms. Not much later on April 24, our company commander Hauptsturmführer Max Kühn was awarded the Deutschen Kreuz in Gold (DKiG or "German Cross in Gold"). After some very long battles, it became very quiet at the front. We arrived in Woltschansk where we set up our new positions in the area of Bjelgorod. Everything was so quiet there which gave us some time to recharge our batteries. But soon we would be engaged in battle again, and we were prepared for the offensive in Kursk. We advanced to the River Mius, and at the beginning of August we were repositioned back to Bjelgorod. In the meantime, we were awarded the Demjansk shield. All our comrades who fought in the Demjansk Pocket were awarded this shield which was worn on the left sleeve of the uniform.

The time spent at the front in August 1943 is engraved in my memory, especially because these were my last engagements with the Regiment "Theodor Eicke", and because I sustained my first war injury there. During our engagement in the area of Nikitowka, we suddenly stood in front of a large piece of wetland. The wetland was very deep, and one could only cross it by use of a wooden bridge. Because of the troop movements, and all the vehicles that drove over the bridge, it totally sunk away in the wetland. I told one of my comrades not to wait to cross the bridge, and to move through the wetland as soon as we could. It was about 300 meters of wetland we had to cross, but on the other side the surface was dry again. We all made it through the wetland without any problems. When we arrived on the other side, we observed a couple wooden houses which were on our left flank, while laying in front of us there was a pile of telegraph poles. Suddenly I heard a shot followed by an impact. Whatever it was it hit the wooden houses and I screamed out because of the pain I felt in my body. I was hit! I yelled at one of my comrades to fire a white flare in the air so that the shelling would stop. We were shelling our own troops! I assessed my wound, and I

From Demjansk to Breslau –
3.SS-Panzer-Division - "Totenkopf"

noticed that I had a big piece of wood sticking in my right thigh. I wasn't able to walk anymore, and I collapsed. I quickly learned that we were shot at by our own Panzer or tanks! A Panzerspähwagen picked me up and transported me to a Kriegslazarett. While in transport, we came under fire of the "Stalinorgeln" or Stalin's Organs/Katyusha. For a moment I thought that this would be the end. On August 14, 1943, I arrived in the Kriegslazarett in Krasnograd. During the night of August 14-15, the Russians started to bomb Krasnograd. We tried to protect ourselves the best we could by hiding in the cellars of the buildings we were in. Because my injury wasn't that bad, I was released on August 15, and together with a couple of other comrades, we received our release papers. Because it was already late in the evening, I was unable to go back to my unit. I had to find a place to spend the night, and as soon as I found something I started to unpack my gear. Suddenly someone knocked on the door, and when I answered the door I saw two members of the Feldpolizei. They asked what I was doing there, and what my plans were. I told them I was going back to my old unit since I had been released from the Kriegslazarett. When they checked my release papers, they noticed that there was no signature from the commander of the Kriegslazarett. I forgot to get his signature when I left, and this was a problem which got me arrested for being absent without official leave. I was taken away by the Feldpolizei. On August 16 or 17, we marched off with six other comrades while being guarded by the Feldpolizei. Our trip took us to Glatz in Silesia. One of the comrades was still unable to walk due to his injuries, and we had to carry him with a little cart. Once we arrived in Glatz, we were put in the local barracks where there were lots of members of the Wehrmacht. The Feldpolizei was all but sociable, and after a couple of days, I was picked up by a truck and transported to Munich-Freimann. The trip to Bavaria was pleasant, and when I arrived in Munich I was placed in a cell but the door remained open which gave me the freedom to wander around in the barracks. After a couple of days, I was informed that soon I had to appear in front of a military tribunal. I believe it was October 3, 1943 that I finally appeared in front of the tribunal. I remember the day before, because Munich was bombed by the RAF which caused a lot of destruction in the city. On my way to the tribunal, I saw the devastation that this air raid had caused. It was horrible! But back to court! Once I arrived in the courtroom, the judge came in and said: "Sturmmann, you're being accused of being absent without official leave from your unit! What do you have to say about this?" I told him the entire story from my arrival in Nikitowka to my arrest in Krasnograd. Now I have to stay that the members of the tribunal were all highly decorated soldiers which worked out in my favor. These men knew about the situation at the front in Russia. The judge ruled to stay the charges, and I was free to go. I was transported back to Munich-Freimann the same day. After a little while I received new marching orders, and I was attached to an Ausbildungskompanie or training unit. Since I was already a veteran, I was excused from training, and I had a good life because the instructors would tell me, "you already know all this stuff, so go sit in that corner and keep your mouth shut!"

I had to do guard duty in the barracks with six other comrades. This wasn't a difficult job at all, and all we did was walk around in the barracks. Every now and then we came in contact with prisoners who had the task of cleaning the barracks. In fact, that was all they did during the day. I spoke to one of them, and he said that life was good in the barracks and that they were all treated very well.

Breslau

In January 1945, I was given some Heimaturlaub again, and I traveled from Breslau to Berlin by train. Once I arrived in Berlin, I traveled north to my parents. My parents didn't know that I was coming home for a bit, and when they saw me they were full of joy. Obviously we had a lot to say to each other. The next day I decided to go for a walk by the POW camp which was located in the former Wehrmacht camp. On the left side of the camp I saw Allied POWs who were always playing some sort of ball games. On the right side there were the Russian POWs. They looked differently as they were so skinny. There was almost no life in their bodies. I talked to a couple of Russians, and they told me that they hadn't eaten for a while now. In fact they were given no food at all, while the Allied POWs got all the food. Another day I visited another camp where there were only Ukrainian women. My mother told me that there was one of the guards who used to beat these women all the time. This guard lived across the street from my parents. I tried to talk to him and told him to be very careful with what he was doing because the Russians would be there soon! Whether he actually listened to me is another thing... After my Heimaturlaub, I went back to Breslau-Lissa. In January 1945, the Russian Army was able to seize two bridgeheads in the southeast of Breslau near Oppeln and Ohlau. The battle for Breslau was inevitable! But even with the Russians being so close it was still very quiet and peaceful in the city. I remember that I went for walks into the city with some comrades, and we visited the old city hall. But while we were on a smoke break, we suddenly observed some high level bombers flying over the city. Before we knew it there were explosions all around us. Apparently the planes started dropping their bombs once they reached the city limits. I was hit by a piece of brick in the head, and I was bleeding like a stuck pig. My comrades immediately took care of my wound, and they brought me to the Lazarett. I still have the scar on my head today! The Lazarett was located in a bunker in the city. Inside there was also a makeshift military court of the Waffen SS. I overheard people talking, and it seemed that they were looking for people to volunteer for a firing squad. As soon as I heard that, I took off. The next day I heard that the firing squad was for an 18 year old Austrian boy who was sentenced to death. We all had to show up for the execution, but when the order was given to fire, I turned my back. I could not understand why they would shoot a young comrade, especially when we were that close to the end of the war. My head wound healed in the meantime, and I had to report for duty with my unit. My unit was posted at the Bahndamm which was the extension of the double tracks from Liegnitz-Breslau. There we were given the orders by an Obersturmführer to form a reconnaissance team for which I picked six comrades. Most of them had no combat experience, but we had to find out exactly where the Russians were at that moment. While we were on our way to look for the Russians, everything seemed to be very quiet at the front. We walked by some houses when suddenly we heard the noise of a tank and a couple of other vehicles. My comrades clearly became nervous, and I had to calm them down. The tank was a Russian T-34 which I had seen before on the Eastern Front. The T-34 was still a safe distance from us. We waited for probably a couple of hours, but then the noise of the engines sounded pretty close. I gave my comrades the order to silently retreat and to stay low. We had to report this to our command as soon as possible. While we were running back to our positions, we encountered five Russian soldiers. One of them had a "Teller-MG" or DPM light machine gun. I started shooting with my MP, and emptied all my magazines. After that I started running for my life, but after 300 meters I stood in front of a very high fence. I can't remember how I crossed that fence, but somehow I managed to get over it very fast and I kept on running. Then I heard a shot from the tank, but it didn't impact in my immediate surroundings. The tank was stopped for whatever reason and remained static. When I reached our positions, there was nothing but chaos. Officers were running around yelling and screaming because they didn't know what to do. The rail yard behind the Bahndamm was crowded with young

From Demjansk to Breslau –
3.SS-Panzer-Division - "Totenkopf"

soldiers. Obviously some of them were very curious about the approaching Russian Army, and they came out of their cover. Just sticking your head out was good enough to get you killed! The first one popped his head out of cover and he was hit by a bullet within seconds. I ran towards the dead soldier and took him away. Not much later, a second one was killed because he popped his head up to see the Russians. I couldn't take this any longer, and I yelled, "Bring me a Panzerfaust!" Clearly there was a Russian sniper looking at our positions from a tree. I could've fought him with my MP40, but that would've been too risky. I was given a Panzerfaust and I looked for a nice position to aim at the sniper. When I found my position, I armed the Panzerfaust, aimed towards the tree, and fired. Next thing you know there was a big explosion and twigs were flying all around. The sniper was gone.

The Russians kept on pushing us back inside the city, and the war became an urban warfare with only house to house combat. Sometimes it happened that a house was occupied by both sides: on the main floor there was us, while the Russians were on the second floor! This urban warfare was very hard for both sides, and many lives were lost there in Breslau. But during my time in Breslau, I never gave up the houses I occupied. Sometimes I stayed inside the same quarter for eight days, and now and then we were able to kick the Russians out again! Together with my comrades, we positioned ourselves on the second floor of a building. From there we had a nice overview of the street, and we positioned our MG34 a little bit more in the back of the room, covered by a big wooden table. We were prepared to receive the Russians now. But on the other side it was suspiciously quiet. Even during the night it stayed very quiet. The following morning some comrades went in search for some food. With the amount of food that they found, we could've easily stayed there for a very long time! In the meantime, a lot of houses were connected with each other through tunnels that went from cellar to cellar. Our "Pioniere" ("engineers") build a complete tunnel network in the city connecting all the houses. When we were encircled by the Russians, there were still a lot of civilians in the city.

In front of our position there was a square which was totally empty. On the other side of the square, there was a big gate in one of the houses from which a Russian 4.5 cm PAK suddenly appeared. One of my comrades yelled, "There's a PAK coming out of the door!" Yes, the Russians used a 4.5 cm PAK which was a copy of our 3.7 cm PAK. I told my MG gunner to wait until the entire PAK passed through the door. Once the PAK was completely exposed, I ordered my gunner to open fire. I only lasted a couple of minutes, and the square was empty again. The PAK was gone again, as it was put back inside the house where it was sitting before. A couple of days later we were moved to another part of the city. It was that part of the city where the River Oder had two "arms." In the middle of the river, there was an island which was already occupied by the Russians. Funny enough, they didn't shoot at us and we didn't shoot at them! Then came the rumor that the Festungskommandant, General Hermann Niehoff, was negotiating with the Russians. We were given the orders to maintain our positions but not to open fire.

Socializing with Russians – the End of the War

We used these quiet days to socialize with the Russians. We told them to come over to our positions, which they did, and what happened then was something that you won't find in any other history books: we embraced each other with tears in our eyes! Just a couple of days before that, we were still fighting each other, and now we were crying together patting each other on the back. We met with our Russian counterparts a couple of times like this, and every time they said, "Woina kaput!" which meant the war is over. Then came

From Demjansk to Breslau –
3.SS-Panzer-Division - "Totenkopf"

the order to gather all our weapons so that we could surrender them to the Russians. When this was done, the long march into captivity had begun. It was a giant waltz of soldiers moving slowly through the streets. While we were marching, a Russian soldier approached a German soldier and wanted to grab his watch. An officer on a horse saw this, approached the soldiers, pulled out his gun, and shot the man right in front of us! We didn't know what happened and why he did that, but we kind of figured out that Niehoff had negotiated with the Russians to leave us alone. The officer turned towards us and said, "Verbotten!" which confirmed that they were respecting the negotiated terms with Niehoff. After several days of marching, we arrived in a camp – a former RAD camp - where there were many other soldiers. We were there with probably 10 to 12 Waffen SS members. We didn't stay there for a long time, and we were split up in smaller groups of 20 men. Every group was guarded by three Russian soldiers. We were marched out of the camp to an unknown destination. After a daylong march, we arrived at a house where we stayed for the night. The next day we were all given a scythe, and we had to start working in the field. Suddenly I heard the bolt action of a rifle. I turned around, and I noticed that one of the guards pointed his rifle at me. Then he put his rifle down and told me to come to him. I carefully approached him while he was lighting a cigarette. When I was close enough, he pushed a cigarette under my nose and told me to put it in my mouth. Then he called the translator whom he told that he was a German POW during WWI, and that he was treated poorly during that time. Then he said that he had no intention to shoot me. You can't imagine how happy I felt on the inside when I heard this. My comrades later told me that when the Russian soldier told me to come to him that my face was as white as chalk. In the following months, we were moved from place to place, and I had no idea where we were until I ended up in Grulich in Sudetenland. It was October 1945, and the rumor was spread that we all would be shipped to Siberia. Now this was the last place on earth where you wanted to go to, so I started talking to a couple of comrades about what our options were. Were we going to Siberia, or would we try to escape? I was able to get six men together, three Waffen SS and three Wehrmacht soldiers, and one day after the evening roll call, we decided to escape. We escaped from the camp, and once we were outside we went down the hill. We kept on running until we arrived at an abandoned farm. There we took a little break, and laid down in a haystack. Early in the morning, we continued our escape until we arrived at a street which looked very familiar to us. Here our group got split up, and the three Wehrmacht soldiers decided to follow their own way. I can't remember how many days we were walking, but we spent every night in the woods. One day we were discussing if we would continue our way through the woods or if we would use the paved roads. It was a dilemma because the woods were safe but not easy to get through, while the paved roads were easier to walk on but not that safe. We finally decided to continue on the paved road, but after 300 meters we encountered three Polish men with MP38s. The next thing we heard was "Hände hoch!" We were all searched and they found my Wehrpass and some promotion documents and award certificates. I think these three guys were more afraid of us than we were of them, and they hastily brought us to the closest police station. I remember the name of the town which was Bad Reinerz in Lower-Silesia. I was separated from my two comrades, and I was transported to Glatz. I knew that town as I spent some time there while I was in military service. We were treated very poorly in Glatz, and we had to stand through the abuse from our guards. One of them took the pleasure of beating us in the back every morning during roll call. When he walked by, we had to turn around so that he could hit us with the rifle butt in the kidney area. This hurt so much that some of the boys were already crying before he actually hit them. When it was my turn, I had enough of his abuse. I turned my back to him and I was getting ready to feel the rifle butt into my kidneys. However when he took a swing at me I jumped away so he missed me. I turned around quickly and I looked him straight in the eyes. He stood completely perplexed, and he didn't know how to react to this situation. He turned around and he ran away. Funny enough, the abuse stopped after this. One day we observed a lot of high ranking officers walking into the camp. They were officers from all of the nations that fought us during the war. They took the time to talk to us, and they told us that we would get the opportunity to speak freely soon. Another thing to mention is that since these officers arrived in the camp, our cell doors would remain open all the time. This way we were able to pay each other a visit and to chat with our old comrades. Then came the day I had had been waiting for, and the chances to go home were very high. But first I had to appear before the courts. On October 8, 1946, I was escorted to a courtroom by a uniformed member. I was provided with a defense counsel who was able to speak German. When the judge came in, I was told to have a seat and listen to him very carefully. The judge asked me how many Polish people I had shot during the war. My answer was sort: "None!" Then they went through some paperwork, and finally the judge said, "Thank you! You are free to go!" I was given my release papers and some money, and I was free to go. When I was on my way back home, I was held in a quarantine camp in Berlin for a couple of weeks, but that was ok with me. I knew I was going home. The camp commander asked me why I wanted to go home, and I showed him a letter from my parents. He said that he would get my release papers in the morning. The way home seemed to be taking forever, and finally I arrived at my parents' home. Obviously my parents were not expecting me at all, so when my mother opened the door, she took me inside to my father and we held each other for a long time without saying a word. I was finally home and the nightmare was over.

The year was 1947.

Soldiers of the Totenkopf Division transporting ammunition in the Demjansk Pocket.

The Panzerjäger of Das Reich

When during WWI our enemies started using armed vehicles, which they called tanks after a while, and they started moving over the trenches and foxholes of our soldiers, there was nothing the German infantryman could do about it. Only heavy artillery was a match for these tanks, as only then could their armor be penetrated. However, our German infantry bravely fought against the French, English, and later the American tanks. Even in the enemy newsreels, they were telling stories about our brave soldiers at the front. There was even an NCO who was mentioned by name in their news as he single-handedly knocked out four tanks with his PAK. He kept firing his PAK until it fell apart. After the war, every army developed its own anti-tank weapons, and in Germany we called them "Panzerabwehrkanonen", or simply PAK. Now everyone knows the PAK which was attached to the Kübelwagen: it was a small caliber PAK with a small barrel, two legs, and the typical rubber tires. The name PAK was a commonly used name, but it didn't do this new weapon any justice. All the soldiers from German PAK units were more than happy when the Führer, in the spring of 1940, gave them a new name: Panzerjäger! That was the correct name for these men, as it did them justice: they wouldn't only defend our troops against enemy tanks, but they would also hunt them down and destroy them. These soldiers, these Panzerjäger, made sure that that the name given to them by the Führer would make them proud. Then the war in the West broke out. The German Panzerjäger bumped into enemy tanks, the 32 ton and the 70 ton French tanks, which they had to destroy. And every time the Panzerjäger were successful in battle: they were able to destroy the enemy tanks or they stopped their advance. The first Panzerjäger to win the Knight's Cross was named Brinkforth, who was a Richtschütze, 14. (Panzerjäger) Kompanie, III. Bataillon, Infanterie-Regiment 25. The Panzerjäger only had one saying during combat: "When tanks attack and when all others run for cover, the Panzerjäger have to stay in their positions and fire back until the enemy is destroyed!"

Into Enemy Territory

Spirited and determined men, these were our SS men of a Panzer Abteilung who started writing history three weeks ago when they marched into enemy territory. The division already advanced for more than 1000 km since the beginning of the campaign. When they crossed the border at Brest-Litovsk, they followed the rest of the divisions over the paved roads. These roads were paved and maintained by the Baukommando. From day two of the campaign, the division was engaged at the front, and their mission was to destroy the enemy vehicles on the terrain. Hidden in the woods and in the swamps were the Bolshevists whose mission was to stop and to sabotage the advance of our troops. But the SS Divisions had already spotted the enemy and fought them back to clear the way. It was there that the SS men learned how the enemy would fight back. When the enemy wasn't victorious in battle, they would retreat, hide, let the SS troops pass by, and then attack them from behind. Also this way they interfered with our supply troops and shot a few of our men. Even the field hospitals had to be protected against their attacks. Or they were hiding in the trees, or they pretended to be dead, but they very much came alive again when our advancing Schützen walked passed them. Others were disguised as simple farmers with farm wagons. In these wagons they were hiding their machine guns and ammunition. But these enemy actions were not able to stop the advance of the SS Divisions. All bridges had been destroyed by the Russians, and on the other side of the river they fortified their positions with artillery. They tried to defend their positions at all costs, however they didn't take into account the heavy German artillery and the Schützen of the SS Divisions! While the other side of the river was being cleared of the remaining enemy forces, the German batteries finished their job. In the early morning, the Schützen of the Waffen SS crossed the river in their rubber rafts. For the Panzerjäger it was a difficult day, as they had to take all their equipment on rubber rafts. Once they arrived on the other side of the river, they had to carry all of their equipment until they reached the woods. In the woods, the enemy was still in position. Through thundershowers they advanced through the woods and pushed back all the Bolshevists while a stronger bridgehead was being built. The next day the troops moved forward, and they fought their way through an enemy fortification in Minsk. Parts of the division pushed through to the north and they were able to destroy a Soviet elite formation during the heavy fighting in the woods. On the left flank and on the right flank were only a few Bolshevist troops left, all spread out in the woods. Soon they became surrounded, and slowly the trap around them closed which led to the Kessel. All were eliminated during this battle, and like a finger pointing forward, this is how the advance of our troops through enemy territory can be described. Of course our troops needed protection during their advance, especially on their flanks.

One night a full Soviet Division was planning to break the columns of the advancing Waffen SS troops. The artillery and Panzerjäger were following the advancing troops at a safe distance. It was when one of the first artillery trucks drove through the town that the Soviets initiated their attack. Coming out of the woods they surprised our troops without question. Obviously there were some losses for us: 5 LKW burned out! However our artillery opened fire, and the Panzerjäger came to their assistance as soon as possible. They took position next to the artillery, and without mercy the rage of the heavens fell directly on the enemy forces. The Soviets tried to seize an important intersection from which they wanted to push through an entire platoon of rifle men and MG men; they positioned themselves right in front of our troops. The distance between them and us was short, but the performance was colossal. Most likely it was an entire regiment, and for a moment it looked like it could become a fierce situation for both sides, but the 3rd Battalion initiated their attack. The sight for them was open, and on the horizon, the town in question, in particular the intersection with parts of the forested area which had been used by the enemy to approach our troops.

Panzerjäger in action in Russia 1941.

The commander of the SS Battalion was not impressed by the enemy's show of force. He treated the entire situation as if it was a practice drill: he sent one company to the right, supported by heavy MG and infantry; in the center, he kept the grenade launchers and PAK; on the left he put another company, with the Panzerjäger leading the way. The motorcyclists were tasked to comb through the woods. The furious firestorm hit the Soviets very hard! From all sides death and destruction rained on them. They desperately ran forward, hoping to get out of this hell as fast as they could, but the rage of our guns gave them no way to escape. Totally confused, they tried to escape. The Richtschützen of the PAK battery and artillery took every single enemy vehicle under fire. Every MG nest was wiped out by our grenade launchers, while the hordes of the charging infantry were all bombed with high explosive grenades (Sprenggranaten). Whatever was left over of the enemy troops just gave up. In a panic, they fled away to the north, followed by the fire of all our heavy weapons.

In the morning, it became clear what carnage had taken place the day before: destroyed weapons, charred horses, abandoned and destroyed equipment, but the worst of all were the dead bodies lying over dead bodies of Soviet soldiers. The loss of life was tremendous. Miles and miles of death and destruction was what our reconnaissance troops reported to our HQ. Some of the Bolshevik troops tried to break through to the south during the darkness of the night, and with help of the cover of the trees in the woods. They hoped to regroup with stronger forces there in the hope to continue the war and attack the German forces from behind. But from this group of soldiers, only a bunch of demoralized men was left over. A small group was able to escape, but the majority stayed behind on the battlefield. Many of them reached the road again during the course of the day, but now they were only armed with white flags, as they had left all their weapons behind. Many of them became POWs.

A few days later, our SS men were shown again how brutal and aggressive the Soviets could be during their attacks. The men had to protect an airfield which they had conquered from the enemy, and which the Soviets were trying to conquer back. This airfield was almost like a small city: besides the hangars, repair shops, and airport buildings, it also had several large buildings and barracks. Most likely, this must have been a place where Soviet pilots and other air force troops had resided before. It was an incredible view because in the midst of the nothingness of the Russian plains, there was this big city. During the night, the SS men stopped the Soviet attack. The next day, our troops marched through the airfield where they observed numerous Soviet planes which had been destroyed on the ground by our airplanes. Without pause, they marched on until they reached their new positions late at night. They didn't know that the following day they would be participating in one of the most brutal and heaviest battles of all battles. It would be something they had never experienced before.

Objective: Jelnya

Early in the morning, the SS Division and a Panzer Division were getting ready to engage: with a major encircling movement, they had to seize the city of Jelnya to secure a bridgehead there. The assault was set up in a particular way that it had to mislead the Soviets. Around the city there were already different motorized Schützen of the Panzer Division; they remained calm and were waiting patiently for orders. To their north, in the focal point of the action, stood three battalions of the SS Regiment, and on their left flank the 2nd Motorized Regiment in stand-by, while the 3rd and some other units were protecting the northern flank. The battalion's first objective the located to the east, the second objective was to the South-East, and the third and fourth to the south. All units had to observe the deadline which was set almost at the minute. Also the timing was set for the pre-attack fire preparations, and the artillery's change of positions. A clock was mounted which had to be observed by all troops for when the signal was given to start the attack.

The attack had started, and if the attack was to be successful, it would chase the enemy out of his fortified/reserve positions in the

The Panzerjäger of Das Reich

famous Stalin Line by means of a new attack to the flank, then rolled up from the side, and then caught from behind. Our young volunteers of the Waffen SS who had already marched 20 km that day in the burning heat of the sun, were more than prepared to fight again under the cover of our artillery, even after executing four previous attacks. From these four previous attacks, three were close-combat fights, while in front of them stood a new and crisp division which had just arrived from Siberia to the front. Even with the numerous swamps and impossible woods to cross, the priority remained that the ammunition would have to pass to the front line even when under heavy enemy fire. No radio station was to be left behind either. The leadership had to be prepared for difficulties which were unavoidable, and which could not always be foreseen. When around noon, the enemy artillery started shelling our positions, the help from above arrived. Our proud birds, the Junker Ju 88, came out of the clouds with heavy bombs to silence the enemy artillery. When the enemy artillery wanted to disturb the push forward of our regiment on the left flank, the Messerschmitt destroyers came out of the clouds like hawks, fighting the enemy with their board weapons. But the most impressive were our dive bombers (Stuka). At the railway embankment, which was the third objective of the attack, the open terrain gave a major advantage to the Bolshevist. Over the open field, our companies had to attack the enemy while being totally exposed. The enemy just had to adjust his weapons/artillery to the meter to get to us. In an aggressive attack, the railway embankment was seized by our troops. Armed with bayonets and hand grenades, we had to take all these Siberians out of their holes. These Siberians were indoctrinated by their abominable propaganda to fight their desperate war against us. But 100 meters behind the conquered lines stood a second line of reserve troops of the Soviet Army. They were hiding in the cornfield, and they were taking our troops under fire. Because of this new enemy attack, our enemies were taken back behind the railway embankment. This bloody game was repeated over and over again until the railway embankment was seized again by our troops. But as soon as the enemy took cover, the sound of the screaming dive bombers could be heard again. Desperately, the Bolshevists fired flares into the air hoping for some back-up to arrive quickly, but it only exposed their positions to the our dive bombers even more! Three to four times, the dive bombers screamed over the battlefield, and then there was that expected silence. Every soldier looked up to the sky; the SS men were full of joy, but with how much fear did the Bolshevists look up to the sky? Once the bombs were dropped and all the sounds had faded away, there were only steep mushroom clouds rising up into the sky. The entire battlefield became quiet for a moment, but soon our MG started rattling again. The railway embankment was finally taken! The last resistance could now be broken, and in the darkness the heights were seized without firing one bullet. Our motorized units to the right and their sister regiment to the left were able to advance to their objective as they were initially ordered. The Panzerjäger had accompanied the attack of the infantry. Even if they didn't have to march all the time, it wasn't always an easy task to drive the Kübelwagen or a half track vehicle with a PAK attached to it. It was actually a difficult piece of work to bring the PAK to the front. Now that the division transitioned into the defensive mode for a short time, the Panzerjäger were split up and assigned to individual battalions. They were a little bit separated from the companies, but they were ready to fight. Their orders were to provide security for the troops.

In a cornfield behind the front lay an SS Regiment, and this included Untersturmführer Roger and his platoon. Every now and then the enemy fired with their artillery, however it didn't bother the Panzerjäger too much. Just shooting or actual fighting were two separate things. Just in case, they had their foxholes ready, but most of the time they were just sitting on their vehicles waiting to see what the day would bring them. The battalion's Zugführer arrived on the scene, and he ordered his men to assemble around him. Immediately the Panzerjäger assembled around him, but the Zugführer didn't begin to speak right away. The Zugführer - Untersturmführer Roger - was a young and blond Egerländer (Bohemia). He was one of those men that just said the things how they were. He looked at his men, to the entire club, as he liked to call them, and he looked every man straight in the eyes. With him were his Halbzugführer; Oberscharführer Siewert and Zink. Both were seasoned soldiers who were decorated with the Iron Cross First Class during the campaign in Poland, during the early days of the war. Then there was Geschützführer Boddien, Stritz, and Zeissig. He knew every man and their history, and for some of them, he had already put his hand into the fire to save their behind. A bit on the side, a bit timid and shy, but very loyal, stood the youngest of our pack, the 17 year old Heinz Reichel nicknamed "Pimpf".

Finally Untersturmführer Roger started addressing his men, "Comrades, something great has happened. The 2nd Company destroyed eight tanks, but what's so great about it is that they were all destroyed by one man: Unterscharführer Rössel. I received the report from his unit that his PAK was positioned on a small elevation and that eight tanks drove towards his position. Uscha Rössel gave the order to let the tanks approach to about 50 meters, and then shoot the first and last one first, and then the rest in between. I have to say that the Geschützführer's order was superb, and an example for all of us. I hope that this event will repeat itself so that we can keep up the standards of the 2nd Company. And the opportunity will present itself again since the Bolshevists are putting new tanks into battle. I'm also pleased to announce that from the POWs, we heard that Radio Moscow and their superior officers are calling us the elite division of the Führer! Keep up the good work! And when the Soviet tanks approach our positions, then we'll show them what the word destruction really means to us! Dismissed!" Actually Ustuf Roger wanted to say more, but within the last minutes the enemy artillery fire had increased significantly. In times like these, he preferred not to have the men gathered around one vehicle or in one place at the time. He went to his vehicle and observed the impacts of the enemy fire. The enemy fire drew itself more and more towards the area of the III Battalion, and seemed to concentrate around that particular area. It looked like a preparation for an artillery barrage. Immediately after Ustuf Roger had heard the alarm from the III Battalion, the artillery fire seemed to calm down. Pimpf, his messenger, stood right beside him. "You think the Bolshevists will storm our positions?" asked Pimpf. "Looks like it. All the MGs are firing," replied Ustuf Roger.

The Panzerjäger and the 52 Ton Tank

In the command post of the II Battalion, there was suddenly a lot of movement. Ustuf Roger observed the Funkers take messages and phone calls while all the others around them seemed to be listening intently. While all the others were listening anxiously to what was going on, the leaders of the command post suddenly heard the call: "Heavy tank broke through the lines of the III Battalion's position!" Ustuf Roger jumped in his vehicle, and in one sentence he yelled, "Geschütz Stitz and Geschütz Bodien, we're going in pursuit of this heavy tank!" Like the wind, the men flew into their vehicles. Pimpf threw himself into the back of the Führerkübel. The drivers started the engines, and they drove off towards the enemy tank. Crosswise they drove through the cornfield and they started their hunting party towards the positions of the III Battalion. Ustuf Roger was standing up straight in his vehicle while he was yelling commands to his troops while they were approaching the enemy tank. The enemy tank was

The Panzerjäger of Das Reich

now at the edge of the cornfield. There the intruder stopped at about 100 meters distant, and slowly turned its turret. Clearly it was looking for a target. "Unload and fire at will!" The first shot was fired, however the projectile bounced off the front of the tank as if one just threw a pea at it. 'It must be a 52 ton tank,' Ustuf Roger thought to himself, however there wasn't too much time to think about it. "Aim between the turret and the hull!" It took a bit longer for the next couple of rounds to be fired, however the gunners were aiming towards the tank with the highest precision now. Shots were fired, and this time the turret stopped moving. Because of the impact of the projectiles, the sides were blown apart and the turret got stuck. The turret was turned to the right and the Bolshevists noticed their bad luck at that moment. Suddenly the tank took off at a high speed in the direction of the town where the regiment was located. "That will give the regiment some fun!" said Ustuf Roger. We didn't follow the tank into the town as there would be enough of our own men waiting for it and we didn't want to jeopardize their security. "They'll know what to do with it. They'll take cover in their foxholes or in the houses. Nothing will happen to them." But the tank drove around the town, turned back, and then stopped on a light elevation. The cornfield gave the Panzerjäger cover and they were quite close to the road which the tank had to take to drive away. "Let him come closer," said Ustuf Roger while thinking about Uscha Rössel. "60 meters...50 meters...not yet...45 meters...not yet...40 meters. Fire at will!" The first shots were fired - more like rapidly fired - at the longer side of the hull which was more vulnerable. Then the shot of shots was fired: straight into the muzzle of the tank's cannon! The tank was completely destroyed now, at least that's what we thought. But the tank kept on driving away in the direction of its own artillery positions. "The hunt continues, boys! Attach the equipment and off we go!" Yes it was a wild hunting party, however the game wasn't ready to give up yet. It was still waiting for the "coup de grace."

"We'll attack in a crisscross pattern," ordered Ustuf Roger. "One PAK fires at the target while one PAK keeps driving and then sets up to fire at the target from another angle. The first PAK will then drive by the target and set up a little further to fire from another angle. This will continue until the tank is destroyed." And this is how it happened. Boddien caught up with the tank while Stitz stayed in the back. Boddien prepared his PAK and took a shot. Stitz continued driving in a crisscross pattern, and prepared his PAK from the other side. Both PAK attacked the tank from a distance of 30 to 40 meters.

Pak 36 in action in Russia.

The PAK grenades penetrated the thick armor, and Stitz was the first one who delivered a decent hit to the tank. He actually hit the beast in the tracks, which immobilized it immediately. "All on this one boys!" yelled Ustuf Roger while he drove in his Kübelwagen to the front of the action. "Bring me the Panzersprengladung!" The driver gave him the 3 kg explosive, and Pimpf was the one who took it from him while jumping out of the vehicle. But the tank wasn't ready to give up yet. Shots were fired from its MG! Luckily the

The Panzerjäger of Das Reich

Panzerjäger all stood in the MGs dead corner so it wasn't able to hit them. But the Bolshevists thought that we would hold off the attack because of their MG fire.

Ustuf Roger was the first one to reach the tank. The Panzersprengladung was attached to the back, and it exploded with a tremendous amount of force. But it didn't have any effects on the tank. Another example of how strong their tanks were. The MG kept firing from the turret. "Bring me an axe!" yelled Ustuf Roger. Halbzugführer Siewert arrived with an axe, and both Ustuf Roger and Zink climbed onto the tank. Ustuf Roger used all his force to whack the barrel of the MG with the axe, taking it out of operation immediately. Zink leaned over the turret and looked at the barrel of the MG and yelled to Ustuf Roger, "That's a nice job!" Zink was a blacksmith by trade before he became a soldier. Both men sat down on the turret while Ustuf Roger ordered one of the Panzerjäger around the tank to bring some gasoline. Most of the Panzerjäger were standing around the tank now with their weapons at the ready. They didn't want to take the chance that the enemy would suddenly jump out of the tank and attack them. Heinz Reichel brought a jerry can of gasoline. "Thanks Pimpf!" said Ustuf Roger while he took the jerry can on board. He poured the contents out over the tank, especially in every hole or crack that was visible. "And now take cover Zink!" The Panzerjäger around the tank took cover, and Roger threw a hand grenade to the tank. A powerful explosion followed but it didn't ignite the gasoline. "Bring me a flare gun!" This one worked quite well, and the tank was engulfed in flames within seconds. Suddenly there was a loud bang and all the men around the tank were lying flat on the ground. A gigantic fireball went up from the tank. The tank looked to be swallowed by the fire. When the fire tempered down, we could see the turret lying next to the hull in the grass. Most likely the gasoline had penetrated the vehicle and lit up the ammunition inside which blew up immediately. "This could have been a lot worse. In the future we all have to take better cover. OK, let's regroup and drive back!" said Ustuf Roger to his men.

However, Ustuf Roger's men were not the only ones who had destroyed a tank that day. At the I Battalion and III Battalion position, more tanks had been able to break through. Some were destroyed by the artillery, and some of them by our tanks. But most of the tanks were single-handedly knocked out by the men. Two or three tanks were able to reach the artillery's position from the back. One of our drivers was able to follow them for about 800 meters, and shot them one by one. It was as if he was a cattle driver on top of his horse trailer, reported one of the men. However one of the funniest things happened to the engineers (Pioniere). They were transporting the rations with their vehicle while driving over the terrain, thinking nothing bad could happen to them, until one time an enemy tank crossed their path. They didn't let the enemy intimidate them and they drove through a cornfield, following the tank until it had to slow down. The men didn't hesitate, and both jumped out of their vehicle armed with grenades. One of them used the barrel of his rifle to open up the latch of the turret and then they threw their grenades inside the tank. The grenades exploded and the tank burned out completely. From the explosion and the smoke, both were covered in a thick layer of soot. They got back into their vehicle and continued on their way. But during their ride, some of the soup that they were transporting was spilled on their uniforms. This gave them quite a funny look when they passed our HQ. The HQ adjutant stopped them and asked them for an explanation as to why they were looking like two idiots. When they told him their story, the adjutant took them to the commander who was again given an explanation about their actions. With their faces still black and their uniforms covered with soup, they were both presented with the Iron Cross

The Panzerjäger of Das Reich

First Class. So our Panzerjäger were not the only ones who were successful that day, however they had the best result. They were able to destroy the so called invincible 52 ton enemy Panzer. The Zugführer was writing his report in his vehicle, a report which he would personally bring to the Battalion. Before doing so, he ordered Stitz and Bodien to get new ammunition at HQ, since they used some of their grenades to destroy that big tank. And one would never know what the next day would bring.

Ammunition Run and Taking POWs

Glowing red, the sun went down in the west when Uscha Stitz with his driver Wilhelm Reichel were driving away to get some new ammunition. Just behind the northern exit of Jelnya should be the combat zone and the road that would lead to HQ, was what the Zugführer had told them. It is a narrow road to reach, but it's easy to find. They had to drive through the combat zone, and they passed the knocked out 52 ton tank which was still smoldering at that time. Just behind the tank, they observed the railway embankment. Because the fastest way to the road was to drive straight ahead, they drove through the unknown terrain. The good thing was that a halftrack vehicle could drive over any terrain. When it drove up a hill or slight elevation, the front wheels would come off the ground just to come back down when just over half of the vehicle moved over the top. They reached the road, but the condition of it was unknown. Parallel to the road to Jelnya was the railway embankment, but the road wasn't comparable to the ones in Germany. In Germany there were driving lanes, sidewalks, etc., but here in Russia the roads were comparable to a simple field road. The roads here were covered with a thick layer of dirt, and there were holes and other irregularities all over; there were no traffic lanes, and sometimes it looked as if there were four to five lanes at the same time. After heavy rainfall, there was so much mud on the roads that vehicles went around the bigger puddles, creating extra lanes. The road to Jelnya was the one the Russian tanks were following, but it was also the place where they met their destiny. Russian tanks were lying all over the place on the side of the road, some of them completely destroyed. Some of them were still burning. They were stopped where the German forces had stopped them forever. One tank was still standing in the middle of the road. When both comrades were driving to Jelnya, they first passed a field hospital. Our tanks were placed around the field hospital to protect our wounded comrades. The road made a turn and then went over a wooden bridge. "Slow down!" yelled Stitz to his driver, "Soon this entire thing will collapse." After the bridge there was the city, but was this actually a city: a couple of wooden houses, and around the market square a couple of stone buildings? Everything was old and not maintained at all. The city looked empty and lots of buildings were burnt down, and one could only see the remaining stone chimneys as a witness of the past. "Let's continue our way through," said Stitz. "We have nothing to look for here, and I don't want to waste my time here." At an intersection stood a Feldgendarm, directing traffic. He was pointing to which direction we had to follow. Soon they arrived at the main supply station, and they continued until they reached their assigned ammunition truck. Uscha Stitz reported their arrival at the company commander, and soon after, he went to get his supplies. The news that a 52 ton tank had been destroyed had already reached the ammunition depot, and from all over the place there were comrades approaching Stitz to congratulate him and to ask questions about that particular tank. But he didn't have too much time to stay and chat with the men there, as he had to go back to his unit. Soon it would become dark, and they had to act fast so they could be on their way back again. The way back was easier, as they knew their way through the city now. Inside the city it was very quiet, and there were no more other vehicles around. Only in the distance one could hear the artillery still firing.

Waffen-SS troops and two Russian partisans/soldiers – location unknown.

Their eyes were fixed on the road now as there were irregularities all over and breaking down here with their vehicle was certainly not an option. They approached the tank which stood in the middle of the road. "Careful," said Stitz after a while, "we're approaching that tank on the road!" While they approached the tank, they observed some movement around the tank. Two dark figures were on the tank. Carefully they drove past the tank when Reichel asked, "did you see those two dark figures Uscha? I hadn't seen them before when we were driving towards the city." "I can't remember seeing them either," Stitz confirmed. "We have to stop." Reichel stopped the vehicle and both men jumped out. While approaching the tank, they observed two peasants lying on the side of the road. Peasants wearing civilian clothes. Were they sleeping there? "Strange they're sleeping on the side of the road in the ditch!" said Stitz. He took his pistol and woke the two up. Both men jumped up very fast, a bit too fast for men that were sleeping. Reichel told them to keep their hands up after which he searched their pockets but found nothing significant. Stitz looked at their faces while lighting them up with his flashlight.

Germania's Assault Generation

Both looked way to intelligent for peasants and one even looked like a Jew. Something wasn't right here. Stitz decided to take these two men into custody when his eyes caught a bag lying on the ground not far away from them. "Reichel, take a look at that bag there," said Stitz. "It's damn heavy Usha" Reichel replied. At that moment, one of the two men brought his head down and charged towards Stitz. Apparently he had calculated his assault very well and Stitz could've shot him without even aiming. But the man didn't get to Stitz, as he blocked the assault by bringing up his left knee and planting it into the assailant's stomach. The man fell down in pain. The other man took advantage of the situation and tried to run away. But Reichel had noticed him, and while the man started running, he punched him in the face. The man went down, and Reichel dragged him by his collar back to Stitz. He threw him on the ground and put his pistol under his nose. Both peasants were tied together and Reichel grabbed the bag and searched it. The bag was remarkably heavy. First a couple of old rags came out together with some bread and bacon. Then more towards the bottom of the bag there was a square box. When taking the box out, it became clear that it was a radio transmitter. These men were not peasants at all, but disguised Soviets who were tasked to spy behind the German lines and transmit their observations through that particular radio. Both men were loaded into the vehicle, and Stitz and Reichel continued their way back to their unit. Without any further incidents, they reached their unit, and both prisoners were brought to the Zugführer. He was of course very happy with the catch of the day, and he ordered to hand these two over to the commander. Now both comrades were able to look for a place to sleep. They used their foxholes which they had dug the day before. The bottom was covered with hay, and if one was lucky he could actually stretch his legs. The Zeltbahn was used as a blanket and the Stahlhelm as a pillow. One more look at the stars in the sky, and both soldiers fell asleep. A bit further down, some sentries were holding guard.

The Russian Counter-Offensive

However at the front lines with the infantry, nobody was sleeping. The Schützen were lying behind their rifles, and all MGs were at the ready. Their eyes were constantly scanning the terrain covered in darkness. On the horizon, in the shrubs close to the birch trees, something was moving. It was a dark spot, something that wasn't there before. The Gruppenführer looked through his binoculars, but nothing was moving now. However the dark spot was still there. Suddenly a sound was heard, like when metal hits metal. Then complete silence again. They were all listening with the highest concentration to the noise. Everything remained calm, and then that sound again...as if someone was crawling over the earth. Again the binoculars were looking around scanning the terrain: in front to the left, at the edge of the cornfield some dark figures were visible. Silently the order was given: "MGs ready towards the cornfield. MGs fire a couple of shots. Fire at will!" The MGs fired and the bullets flew through the darkness of the night. Some of the corn plants were moving. Shortly after that, a man joined the Gruppenführer. It was the Zugführer. "What's going on?" – "Enemy reconnaissance troops at the edge of the cornfield. Looks like they're gone Ustuf." From the railway embankment close to the neighboring platoon, MG fire was heard as well. Flares went up and came down again like the grenades of a mortar. Some rifle shots were heard and then...silence. "That was another attempt," said Ustuf Roger, "and we have to careful." Then he continued his way to one of the groups positioned a bit farther down. There was a little pathway/ditch which led to the neighboring companies. This connection to the others was protected by our reconnaissance troops to make sure nobody could come in.

Germania's Assault Generation

At the crack of dawn, it became rather chilly. At the Panzerjäger's positions, the Zugführer's driver bent over Heinz Reichel's foxhole. "Pimpf, wake up. Move it. Time for guard duty!" Heinz woke up and was wide awake immediately. He was the one with the last shift on guard duty. He was actually given this last guard duty by his comrades so that he was able to sleep through the entire night. Heinz put his Stahlhelm on his head, wrapped his Zeltbahn around him, and took his rifle. "Where shall I go?" he asked. "From the road to Geschütz Boddien. Until now it has been pretty quiet." At a slow pace, Heinz went to the edge of the road to start his patrol. In the east, the sky was coloring red already. Soon the sun would come up, but he knew that before long the Soviet artillery would wake up, and then their first morning greeting would follow soon after that. At Geschütz Boddien he met with the other sentry. Every post had at least one guard on duty. One of the comrades reached over his canteen: "From last night...drink some Pimpf, it's really good tea." It was a nice gesture, and even in the heat of the battle, there was still real tea and coffee prepared for the troops. But the sand in the water from the local wells which grinded the teeth after drinking it reminded us that there was still a war going on. Suddenly artillery shots were heard in the distance. "Enemy fire," said Pimpf. The men heard the grenades whistling over their heads. Then a mushroom cloud rose up from behind the village, and a few seconds later the sound of the explosion was heard. "About 200 meters behind the village," said Heinz. Both ended their guard duty immediately. The Soviet artillery apparently had received new ammunition last night. It wasn't just one shot that was fired, because soon an entire barrage came down on the terrain. They knew the terrain very well since they abandoned it only three days ago, so they knew where to throw their bombs. First they directed their fire towards the regiment HQ, then the road, and then the artillery's positions. The enemy's four batteries were now in action. 'This could become a dangerous situation when they start this early in the morning,' Pimpf thought to himself. He looked at his watch - another 15 minutes before waking the others. The sun was already up now, and one had a clear visual over the heights now, as well as on the positions going all the way to the left to the railway embankment up to Jelnya and the woods. We didn't know if there were still Bolshevists in the woods or not. A motorcycle with side car was started. It was Rottenführer Kollo, who was going to the field kitchen to get the morning coffee. "Good morning Pimpf! Were you also freezing last night? It was damn cold last night." Heinz didn't answer the question, but rather pointed towards the sky. He had spotted something! "Look, airplanes are coming. Those have to be ours!" shouted Pimpf. "Yes they are," said Kollo while was sitting on the saddle of his motorcycle. "Those are the dive bombers, the Ju 87 Stuka!" What a pleasant surprise that was. Immediately the enemy artillery was quiet, as they didn't want to expose their positions to the dive bombers. Pimpf was so excited that he ran to the Zugführer. "Ustuf, dive bombers are coming in!" The Zugführer looked at the sky and so was the entire platoon. They counted: "6, 9, 15,… there another 3! 18 planes!" The dive bombers flew over our positions towards the enemy. Now everyone had seen them, and all were standing straight up looking at the sky. The planes flew in formation one after the other. In all tranquility, they lined up next to each other, and then one by one took a straight dive down until we couldn't see them anymore. Then suddenly they reappeared, flying straight up to the sky. One after the other performed this ritual, and one could see the bombs coming down, immediately followed by an explosion. This ritual was repeated several times and then MG fire. The Ju-87 were shooting with their board cannons now. That was their goodbye. All planes regrouped and flew away in formation over our positions. That was a welcome help, and the Panzerjäger saluted their comrades of the sky. "Thank you fly boys! Please come back soon!" As soon as the planes were gone, the enemy artillery started their barrage again. However both batteries on the edge of the forest remained silent. They had been destroyed completely. Therefore, the Soviets put their 15 cm batteries into action, and soon we had to come into action ourselves. This game continued the entire morning, and there was no doubt that the Bolshevist were planning a new attack. Most likely they resupplied with ammunition, and had new batteries in place. But our Luftwaffe was present and ready to go. The different groups of planes came every two hours, and in between, the Messerschmitt fighters who wrecked the enemy positions even more. As soon as the planes showed up the Soviets became very quiet. Then the SS men came out of their foxholes to stretch their legs. And when the planes were gone, the artillery woke up again. The planes' targets were the enemy positions in front of the II Battalion, and the Panzerjäger observed how medics were running back and forth, hauling in the wounded. Then a bomb came down in the middle of their positions, and debris and people were flying all over the place.

Around 1000h a Kübelwagen arrived. It was the company commander. Ustuf Roger and the commander exchanged some words. They had lots of time to talk to each other since our planes were on a bombing spree again. So for the next 15 minutes everything was quiet and relaxed on our side. "Uscha Stitz!" yelled Ustuf Roger. "Uscha Stitz report to the Ustuf immediately!" repeated the men. Stitz who was standing at his PAK watching the planes, heard the message and prepared himself to go to his superior. He put his buckle on and placed his helmet perfectly on his head. When the old man is present you better look sharp! Stitz ran towards his superior immediately. "Uscha Stitz at your service, Sir!" "Stitz" said the commander, "from your Zugführer I was given a report yesterday about the capture of two enemy soldiers. You did an excellent job!" Then he paused and took something out of his bag. "Uscha Stitz, in name of the Führer and with the approval of your commander, I'm presenting you the Iron Cross Second Class for bravery shown in front of the enemy." The commander opened his hand and there it was, attached to the black white red ribbon, an Iron Cross with a nice and shiny silver edge. The commander attached the medal personally to Stitz' uniform. The Zugführer also shook Stitz' hand and said, "You deserve it, comrade." That was one of the most beautiful moments for Stitz. 'I'm going to write home about this,' he thought. "He said I deserve it, and he called me comrade and this in the presence of the commander! This was our Ustuf Roger, and all I've learned so far is thanks to him. Without his leadership and example, I wouldn't have this Iron Cross." Stitz turned around and went to his comrades who all came to him. The men were standing around him, and they congratulated him. They also wanted to carry him around on their shoulders, however there were the planes again, and the Zugführer ordered all the men back to their foxholes. And the Zugführer was right, because as soon as the planes were gone, the artillery started firing again, but this time with all their batteries. Now they were also engaging their heavy mortars, and a little later we could hear the rattling sound of their heavy MGs. The Panzerjäger were safe in their foxholes, but the fun was over when a messenger arrived from the Battalion HQ with new orders: "Panzerjäger – move to the positions of the 7th Company as soon as possible." Ustuf Roger was already standing in his Kübelwagen, "Attach the equipment and follow me!" And off we went. For five seconds our platoon looked like a beehive, but soon we were behind our Zugführer driving through potato fields and cornfields.

Pimpf was standing on a slight elevation and gestured to stop by putting his hand in the air. "Stop and dismount!" The Zugführer who had left him behind was looking at the positions on the front line. Now we had to continue on foot. Many times we had to lay down when grenades were exploding around us, but after each of these delays, the pace was set higher. With our lungs filled with smoke, we reached the 7th Company where all PAKs were set into position. From this spot, we could clearly see what was going on. From the woods we saw the Bolshevists charging our lines. Brown rows of men stormed out of the woods yelling, "Hurrah!" "Don't fire yet. Let them come closer!" And closer and closer they came, row after row. Soon the third row was storming out of the woods as well. Then the trees behind the enemy infantry started moving and several trees were coming down. These had to be approaching tanks! Indeed they were, because soon they became visible. One tank was firing its MG in short bursts as we could clearly see the muzzle fire, but strangely enough the bullets didn't reach our positions. "They're shooting behind their own lines! This is what kind of people they are!" yelled the Zugführer. Now the Bolshevists were 500 meters from us when we heard shots being fired and the grenades were flying over our heads. These were our troops firing at the enemy. "Our artillery is shooting at them!" the men told each other. The impacts of the projectiles could be seen as they hit the woods in front of us. "Perfect! Now the enemy was caught in between two fires!" The advance of the Bolshevists started to slow down significantly and the second line caught up with the first and the third was approaching them fast. 400 meters - the enemy artillery was getting weaker. The heavy batteries were already silenced. 300 meters - Now some of the enemy batteries started firing again. 150 meters - "Fire at will!" All hell broke loose on the front line where the II Battalion was located. The MGs were rattling as the Schützen were looking for targets, while the mortars were firing at the same time. The Panzerjäger were shooting with high explosive grenades into the brown hordes. They were clearly not thinking about pushing forward anymore, and what wasn't hit remained in fear on the ground and became the victim of shrapnel or other debris that was flying around. At this point in time, they started running out of the woods as there was no discipline and cohesion anymore. Through the binoculars one could see the commissars in between the troops, encouraging them to move forward while they were holding their sword and pistol in their hands. Funny enough, they never crossed the 250 meter line which was now set by the hellfire of the II Battalion.

The enemy tanks took their way on the 7th Company now. "Shoot the tanks! Bring in the anti-tank ammunition!" ordered Ustuf Roger. Now they only had to aim and lock their target. The tanks were still at 400 meters distance which still made them small targets. The first shots only hit them sporadically. Then the tanks turned sideways and disappeared into the terrain. The Soviet attack was stopped, and to complete their defeat, the sounds of roaring engines in the sky could be heard. German planes were on their way, but this time it was the Ju 88s with heavy bombs on board. The Ju 88s dropped their deadly cargo over the woods, after which they turned away to fly into enemy territory to look for more targets. Again the enemy artillery was silent. From both battalions the Soviets had used for their attack, only a few men made it back. Ustuf Roger was concerned about the tanks that had disappeared. Where were they? Therefore he called the Battalion HQ when the news came in from the 5th Company that between the fifth and the neighboring battalion, five enemy tanks were able to break through the lines and were moving towards the railway embankment.

Let's Go on a Tank Hunt!

"Let's go on a tank hunt!" yelled Ustuf Roger. The equipment was attached to the vehicles whose engines were already running. "Off we go!" To find the enemy, to hunt the enemy, and to destroy him, that was the task of the Panzerjäger. Ustuf Roger left Geschütz Boddien at the disposal of the battalion while the rest took off at a high speed. Soon they arrived at the railway embankment, but here were no tanks there. Behind the railway embankment, they discovered - at a distance of approximately 500 meters - two smoke clouds. They went to check things out, and discovered two burning tanks. Two Schützen were standing around the tanks - SS men from another unit. Both had a big smile on their face. "We destroyed them!" said one of them. "We jumped on them and poured gasoline on them, and with the use of a simple match we lit them up. However somewhere over there in the forested area there should be another one." Ustuf Roger observed that both tanks were of the lighter type, and didn't pay any more attention to them. "Follow me!" He drove around the area where the tank was possibly located. The enemy tank had noticed the Panzerjäger and left its cover position, firing constantly at them in the hope of protecting itself. "Unload the equipment and load the guns! Wait to fire until my command!" Ustuf Roger observed the tank driving at a high speed which made it difficult to hit it. At about 100 meters away, it was clear that the tank was not the heavy 52 ton model, but the lighter 32 ton version. "Aim at the tracks!" ordered Ustuf Roger. The Richtschützen brought their PAK into the right angle, and now they were just waiting for the command to fire. But Ustuf Roger was calmly waiting for the tank to come closer. 80 meters, 50 meters...again he thought about Uscha Rössel's tactics...40 meters...now - no not yet...30 meters. "Fire at will!" Three shots were fired at the same time, and all were concentrated at the left of the tank. It was a direct hit, and the track was broken. The sound of grinding metal could clearly be heard. The Panzerjäger were prepared this time: gasoline, hollow charges, and grenades were all ready. Oscha Siewert ran forward, and threw a 3 kg Sprengladung under the tank. A big explosion followed five seconds later, and the tank started burning in the front.

The Panzerjäger of Das Reich

Bundesarchiv, B 145 Bild-F016221-0016
Foto: o.Ang. | 1941/1942

Knocked out Russian T-34 Tank.

Ustuf Roger approached the tank and knocked on the back to let the Bolshevists prepare themselves to come out and surrender. However, he held his pistol at the ready. The latch opened but not a head was seen, but a pistol. A couple of shots were fired by the Panzerjäger, and a bloody hand fell back into the tank, and the latch was closed again. Uscha Schultheiß arrived with his men carrying hollow charges. The men took cover, and they heard five dull explosions. The tank crew had chosen to die. The Panzerjäger were coming out of their cover when a Krad approached their position. It was Oscha Zink who was looking for the other tanks. At the edge of the woods, 500 meters to the east of the railway embankment, he had discovered one, and for a while he had been monitoring it. Ustuf Roger ordered Uscha Zeißig to attach the equipment and to engage the enemy. For this tank he wanted to spare some PAK ammunition. Ustuf Roger made up an assault team with Oscha Siewert, Uscha Stitz, and Schultheiß, and three of their men. They carried gasoline and hollow charges through the undergrowth, and approached the enemy tank. When they arrived at the tank, the latches were all locked from the outside. A new type of Bolshevist tank? They calmly poured out two jerry cans out on top of the tank and attached the hollow charges. "Take cover! Quick!" A loud explosion followed, and the tank was set on fire. "Number two today!" said Ustuf Roger. "Let's go home boys, or is there another one crawling around here in the area?" From the artillery came the message that they had observed a tank approaching the village, however they received such a warm welcome there from the PAK that they opted to turn around. It was a 32 ton tank. It was driving through the field when it had noticed the Panzerjäger. At high speed, it was approaching Geschütz Stitz. One shot after the other was fired from its cannon. Stitz' men took cover behind the protective shield of their PAK, but a piece of shrapnel hit Oberjäger Daus. He fell down as he was hit in the back, however he was not seriously wounded. At the same time, the Panzerjäger opened fire and aimed between the turret and the hull of the tank, hoping to silence its cannon. 20 meters was the distance left between them and the tank so now they had the perfect aim. The turret locked and the tank made a sudden turn 10 meters away from them, directing itself to our artillery. But our artillery was prepared, and they started a barrage at the tank while it was approaching them. The tank was hit, and it broke one of its tracks. It was immediately immobilized, but the Panzerjäger had been following the tank as they didn't want to let go their prize. They had no more gasoline, but they still had many hand grenades and some hollow charges at their disposal. When they approached the tank, its MG started firing. "Stop! Take cover and make sure to beat that death factory with an axe!" This time only Pimpf thought about bringing an axe. "You're a golden boy!" said Ustuf Roger while taking the axe. Ustuf Roger, Siewert, and Zink climbed on the tank and knocked out the MG barrel. In the meantime, the other had attached five hollow charges with five hand grenades tied around each one of them. All five were detonated at the same time. This was the end of the tank, as it was engulfed in flames. The MG ammunition inside went off, and then a loud bang. The fire had hit the cannon's ammunition. Happily the entire club went back home. What a day! Their deployment, their discipline, but most of all, their camaraderie was remarkable and an example for all. The Bolshevists lost all their appetite to fight the Waffen SS with their tanks. In two days, 51 Soviet tanks from two regiments were destroyed. As long as these Waffen SS men were at the front, there were no more Soviet tanks around. Schützenkönig was Ustuf Roger who was able to destroy the 52 ton tank and many of the 32 ton tanks. When the cauldron around Smolensk was breached, the surrounded Soviet armies destroyed, and every pocket of resistance silenced, the message came from the division that the men of Ustuf Roger fought with the greatest distinction. The men of Ustuf Roger's unit were utterly proud that their Zugführer was serving with the bravest of the bravest.

Götterdämmerung – the Last Moments of the 33.Waffen-Grenadier-Division der SS - "Charlemagne"

Krukenberg and his men already had commenced retreat. The streets were filled with rubble and vehicle wreckage, but still, the retreat went on without much difficulty. Before they were to cross the river, Krukenberg sent two officers to scout ahead. None of them returned. At 0300h, May 2, 1945, Krukenberg decided to go out on reconnaissance himself, with only his escort. Along the way, he met up with SS-Brigadeführer Ziegler. There were a couple of Knight's Cross recipients among them, including Eugene Vaulot. Meanwhile, dawn came, exposing the retreating soldiers to enemy fire. Trying to avoid it, they headed down Gesundbrunnen towards Pankow, and further on towards Wittenau. The column moved slowly on Brunnenstrasse. It again came under mortar fire on Lortzingstrasse. The men were able to find feeble protection under the ruins, but the attack was growing in strength. Ziegler, who was right at Krukenberg's side, was hit by shrapnel and died instantly. Others suffered injuries. They decided to rest for a little while and recoup. The French and Scandinavian Waffen SS volunteers, however, were concerned that if they stay there for any length of time, they could expose the Berliners hiding there to danger. They chose to move on, and went straight under fire from snipers. With nowhere else to go, they went back towards the center of the city to plan their next move. To increase their chances of getting out of Berlin's hell alive, Krukenberg and his men decided to take off their uniforms and put on civilian clothing. It was close to 1000h, May 2. Dressed as civilians, the group went north on Schonhauser-Allee. As they moved away from the city center, they passed one Soviet patrol after the next. So far, no one bothered them. The Russians were busy watching windows in the surrounding townhouses, expecting to be ambushed by the enemy lying in wait there. In the Pankow quarter, Krukenberg went inside a house to change clothes. When he came back outside, none of his fellow soldiers were there. There was a woman there, however, and she told Krukenberg that all his comrades were taken prisoner by the Russians. On the other side of the street, he could see two more Ivans. Krukenberg managed to tempt them with his wristwatch, and in the small chaos that ensued, he was able to disappear towards Schonholzer Park. There, he spent over an hour looking for his men, to no avail. This confirmed his fear that all of them really were taken. Krukenberg continued on alone, heading towards Wilhelmsruhe. Around 1300h, he was stopped and arrested by a Soviet artilleryman.

Having crossed the River Spree, those who went ahead of Krukenberg, divided into smaller groups to avoid attention of the Russians. Each of these groups had, more or less, 15 to 20 men. Wilhelm Weber, the Kampfschule's CO, was there and about twelve of the Frenchmen, including Appolot, Vaulot, and Waffen-Rottenführer Evrard, and a few Germans and Scandinavians. They moved westward with the support of two Tiger tanks. They managed to cross the Tiergarten, but they met with a heavy enemy patrol. The tanks were able to push ahead, but the men dispersed. Eugene Vaulot, decorated with the Knight's Cross just days before, was killed by a sniper. Evrard followed Weber because he believed he had better chances with a German leading the way, as opposed to a Frenchman unfamiliar with Berlin and the surrounding areas. Weber gave the order to get to the nearby buildings as quickly as possible, but soon enough they became surrounded. Their situation turned from bad to hopeless. They were able to hold off the Reds for a few hours before they decided to try and escape. A few of them managed to get through the Soviet net, but not all were as lucky. Two grenadiers, Francois de Lannurien and Jean Clause Dautot, were meanwhile still at the Stadtmitte station. They were the only Frenchmen to stay there after Krukenberg and his unit had left. Both were injured, and so they decided to stay behind, believing they wouldn't be able to get very far anyway. Dautot was severely wounded and suffering so badly that de Lannurien decided to take him to the closest first aid station, in the Reich's Chancellery. With much difficulty, they reached the Führer's bunker on the Vosstrasse. Dautot was taken away on a stretcher to one of the field hospitals, and de Lannurien was patched up. Unfortunately, no one there was able to remove the shrapnel from his hand, which was hurting him more and more. He was left alone, feeling deeply forlorn. He chose to go back to Stadtmitte, hoping to find some of his friends. He found no one there, and joined a random group of soldiers led by a Tiger tank. Combat experience told de Lannurien that it wasn't a good idea to move too close to the tank, as the machine was always a good target for the enemy to aim at, and so he walked about 20 meters away from the rest of the group. He was right to do so! Soon enough, the tank suffered a direct hit. The force of the blast threw de Lannurien to the ground, and instantly killed those who were closest to the tank. According to him, Reichsleiter Martin Bormann was among them. A piece of shrapnel practically removed his head from his body. De Lannurien ran to Stadtmitte. Once there, he found only disappointment and one young German SS-man, desperately firing off his heavy machine gun. The Frenchman proposed to be the shooter's gun loader. After dispensing all of their ammo, they went down to one of the basements to await the inevitable. A few minutes later, they both were taken prisoner by a Soviet patrol. After the war, de Lannurien claimed to have met Hitler himself in the Chancellery, and that the Fuhrer went up to him and congratulated him on his courage when he saw the three-colored shield on his uniform. This seems quite unlikely, however, and unconfirmed by anybody else. What did those last moments in Berlin look like for the wounded Jean-Marie Croisille? Let us hear from him once more: "The aid station, where they hauled me off to, was really a small private clinic. The doctors disappeared somewhere, leaving only two or three nurses, Belgians, shipped here for work. Fire could already be heard on Bulowstrasse. The Ivans are close and the nurses are clearly getting ready to run. I lay on my back on the bed and not move. I'm completely numb. I'm so tired that, despite the noise and tumult around me, I simply fall asleep. Or lose consciousness, it's hard to tell. When I open my eyes, I'm surrounded by Soviet soldiers, rifling through my pockets, taking or destroying everything they find there: papers, my soldier's book, some change, photographs...I pass out again. In my half-dream I feel myself being dragged and moved. Don't know by whom. I sleep or maybe I'm unconscious, I don't know...Nothing seems to be able to wake me, like Labourdette that morning...When I finally come to, I find myself on a table in some hair salon. Next to me, a German soldier, wounded in the leg. The ceiling is made of glass and through the charred panes I can see fire. It's awfully hot. The salon is starting to burn. The two of us, the German and me, support each other and manage to get out onto the street. So I'm not, in fact, paralyzed as I had feared, just numb and in shock. And there still is that odd, hard to describe feeling, as if legs and my arms were not quite mine. And, again, we get to that hellish Mannsteinstrasse. The buildings there are full of the Soviets, plundering. What they can't carry off with them, they destroy. They don't pay any attention to us, too busy searching the apartments and chasing women whose screams come from everywhere, from apartments and broken up shops. Suddenly, we're stopped by a slant-eyed tank-man, his arms covered up to the elbows in watches, his fingers heavy with golden bands and rings. He's waving his pistol around, pointing at my uniform jacket: "Ha, ha, SS! Skolko ty Panzerfist?" They're still obsessed with the Panzerfausts and he fires off a shot right next to my ear. "Ja, SS, pow pow!" And he shoots again, next to my other ear. We're so sure he's gonna kill us, we don't even react, me and my new friend. In that moment, it'd be easy to die, to top off our defeat in this war. During battle, even though we had no hope for success, there wasn't any time to think and reminisce. You have to go through something like that yourself to understand what it's like to fight when all is lost, when it seems like you're fighting alone against the entire world. When the battle ends, there's only emptiness void of hope or will. It passes after a few days. We sit down on a free bed. Even here, among the wounded, there are men who think we'll get rescued and freed, that it's the Russians who are surrounded in Berlin! A Soviet officer with an escort comes in the evening to officially take a couple dozen wounded soldiers into custody: those that still live (some of the beds only have corpses in them). The officer only wants to take those that can stand on their own feet, me among them. We are escorted away to a nearby building, where they put us all into one small room, packed like sardines. It's so crowded, I even manage to catch some shut-eye, while standing. There are many soldiers here, but also civilians, Schupos policemen, a director of a train station, a red hat on his head, a postman and, generally, anybody in any kind of uniform (no shortage of those in Germany!). The civilians are mostly NSDAP members who were already turned in. They chase us out at dawn! It's April 29. They file us into a long column and march us south, guarded by a few ruffians armed with some museum-quality junk. Along the way, we see scenes of plunder and looting. We pass by unending columns of horse-carriages, trucks, and tanks. We see Mongols and Siberians, trying ride bicycles. We pass a beautiful American convertible, filled with Soviet officers, driving down the street on metal rims, no tires, screeching and sending sparks

Götterdämmerung - the Last Moments of the 33.Waffen-Grenadier-Division der SS - "Charlemagne"

everywhere. There were also a lot of women in uniform. Two days later they transported me to Lichtenrade, to a children's clinic turned into a military hospital. As I entered, all nearby bells started to ring. It was noon, May 3. All that was left of Berlin's garrison, surrendered. The battle for Berlin was over."

The Downfall

What was going on with Henri Fenet and his men during that time? The night of May 1-2 passed by rather calmly for them, if you could even use that word to describe the last moments of the capital's defenders. They were still hiding in the Ministry of Security. By the end of the night, the Frenchmen went outside again to see what was going on. They sent out patrols that, beyond a doubt, confirmed that the last defensive positions were deserted on both sides. A little while later, another patrol brought alarming news that the front line was now by the Ministry for Aviation, on the corner of Wilhelmstrasse and Leipzigerstrasse, literally inches from the "French" lines. Fenet decided to go there, the last bastion of resistance in front of the Reich's Chancellery. They managed to get there without much problem and meet with the Luftwaffe soldiers. Before the Frenchmen could take up positions, they saw, as if in a dream, oncoming cars flying white flags! In those cars, sitting side by side, they saw German and Soviet officers. What was going on? Then unarmed Russian officers showed up, offering cigarettes. A few of the Luftwaffe soldiers took them up on their friendly offer, and soon engaged in lively conversation with the now apparently former enemy. A Major of the Luftwaffe, leading the defense of the building, spotted Fenet and informed him of their plans to surrender. He added that the capitulation was already official, and that it was all over. Fenet could not believe it. It was impossible! Despite their enormous sacrifice and valor, they still had lost. He decided he had to see with his own eyes what the situation in the Chancellery was. He

199

thought that if there was any chance to defend even the smallest section of the ground, they had to do it. Besides, staying in the Ministry for Aviation was foolhardy, and as good as letting themselves be captured. And so they took their guns, ammunition, and their Panzerfausts, and they left the buildings, ignoring yells from the Russians to put their weapons on the ground. The city was eerily quiet. Civilians and unarmed soldiers milled about on the streets. To avoid patrols, the Frenchmen hid in the ruins. Pierre Rostaing was walking last. Deep in his thoughts, he didn't hear nor see the Russian following close behind him, who finally yelled to drop his weapons and to put his arms up. The Frenchman didn't respond; only ran towards his friends. The whole incident ended without a shot being fired. Rostaing joined Fenet and the rest later, as they marched through the ruined silent city. They entered the tunnels through the air vents, where they had the best chance to reach the Chancellery unseen. Along the way, they passed by the Stadtmitte station, Gustav Krukenberg's former command post. Not a single soul there. They moved on towards Kaiserhof station, in front of the Chancellery. When they got there, they saw a ladder leading up to the air vent and out to the surface. Pushing through the pain of his leg, which wasn't yet healed, Fenet started climbing up. He expected to hear sounds of battle, but the only noise coming from the surface was the sound of cars driving above. This gave him pause. What was going on up there? A few rungs more. Finally, he could see what was happening, and he could not believe it. Russian soldiers, tanks and other vehicles were everywhere. The Chancellery was in ruins, her facade riddled with artillery missiles and other, smaller caliber bullets. Not a German soldier in sight. It really was all over. He discovered and saw an entirely new world, so much different from what they've just been through and which, seemingly, was already slipping into oblivion. He went back down without a word. His men were eager to hear what he had to say. Fenet told them the Russians were everywhere, and the

Götterdämmerung - the Last Moments of the 33.Waffen-Grenadier-Division der SS - "Charlemagne"

Fuhrer was sure to be dead. They all hung their heads. Some despaired. Without the slightest noise, the Frenchmen went to the Potsdamer Platz station. With much difficulty, they passed through caved-in tunnels, making their way with bayonets or even bare hands. But they moved onwards. On Potsdamer Platz another unpleasant surprise awaited them. The scouts reported the tunnel was ending and leading up to the surface! Day was in full, and in the light it was impossible to go forward and remain unnoticed. They decided to divide into smaller groups and disappear. They went back to the tunnel to wait for nightfall. One of the tunnels ran under an archway of a bridge. It was collapsed, and the rubble and various object provided excellent cover. A few of the older men from the Volkssturm who were nearby decided to hide there as well. Making too much noise, they attracted attention from an enemy patrol. They started yelling "Don't shoot, don't shoot!" which only provoked the Russians into a more careful search of the area. The French groups, one by one, were discovered. One of those groups comprised of, amongst others: Fenet, von Wallenrodt, Douroux, Georges, and Bicou. They hid behind a pile of wicker baskets. With their hearts in their throats, they saw the Reds take their comrades prisoner. The Russians continued their search. Hearts pounding, the Frenchmen held their breath, as the Ivans passed by. On several occasions, one enemy would come close to the baskets, but not search them. Ten meters away, their friend, Fink, was taken by the Soviets, screaming: "Surrender like National Socialists!"

From his hiding place, Fenet observed the situation. He saw a Russian officer count the captives. He looked at his watch. Only an hour had passed! When will this night come! After a while, the sounds of steps moved away, and then came back again, accompanied by voices in conversation. There were more the Russians now, and they were coming back! This time they were checking everything even more carefully, and yet they missed the Frenchmen, huddled next to one another like quarry, twice! They still believed they could elude capture. The end came suddenly, however.

With the butts of their guns and their boots, the Russians broke through the wicker baskets and jumped the surviving SS-men. They took them at gunpoint, first freed them of their watches, and then their weapons. It was May 2, 1945, after 1500h. Pierre Rostaing, who was with another group, thus describes the moments before capture: "The Russians attacked the metro. We pushed through the darkness of the tunnels, firing left and right. Only screams of pain let us know if we hit anybody or not. Finally, we got out onto the surface, heaving, at the end of our ropes. The small metro station appeared before us, just 200 m ahead. No sign of life. The platform was covered with huge baskets, easily fitting a man. We spent the night there. The stillness and quiet moved us to reflection. All my life passes before my eyes, as if on a movie screen. I see my engagement, my wife and my daughter who remained in Grenoble and left me, unable to understand the purpose I set my life to. I think of my father who died when I was in Russia and, because of that, the funeral I couldn't attend. My poor mother who had died long before all of this. Now I am alone, except for my sister and two brothers, who'd probably forgotten me already. I could die right here but it's stronger than me, this incredible will to live, just like the other sixteen survivors of "Charlemagne", who are here with me. The small station slips into the night. We took apart our weapons and scattered the pieces. They tore off the SS badges from our collars, leaving only our rank insignia, knowing what was to happen to us. We fell asleep. Suddenly, we're awoken by a voice: "Give up or we'll blow the station!" We didn't respond. The voice repeated the order in French. We look at one another. What was to do? We no longer had any weapons. This time the battle for Berlin ended for us for real. We

Götterdämmerung - the Last Moments of the 33.Waffen-Grenadier-Division der SS - "Charlemagne"

were only left with the satisfaction that we did fight until the end. It is May 2, 1945, around midnight. The prisoners were led outside. Truckloads of singing Russians playing accordions keep driving through Potsdamer Platz. The majority of the fresh victors are completely drunk. One Russians, passing by, yelled "Hitler kaput!" Von Wallenrodt, a bitter smile on his face, replied, "Ja, Hitler kaput." Another Ivan described in lavish details the charms of Siberia waiting for them. Other Russians would shoot imaginary guns at them, screaming: "SS...Pow! Pow! Kaput!" Noticing Fenet's limp, another Russian told his comrade off for just injuring his foot and not blowing the Frenchman's head off. "The dance of the scalp is on."

The guards gathered up the prisoners to march them onwards. Albert Brunet marched next to Henri Fenet. A drunk Popoff grabbed his armed and tried to drag him towards one of the building but a guard quickly realized what was going on, and got Brunet back to the column. He said to Fenet: "I'd have very slim chance for escape." The drunken Russian wasn't about to let him off, though. He wanted revenge. He screamed: "SS, SS!" and fired at Albert Brunet at close range. The Frenchman fell to the ground at Fenet's feet with a hole in his head. Was that the fate of them all? The guards quickly moved the column forward. They passed by the Reich's Chancellery, their last bastion and last hope, which was now being looted by the Red Army. Hundreds of tanks with red flags paraded from the Tiergarten to the Brandenburg Gate, their misshaped forms rising defiantly to the grey sky. The prisoners passed by the Chancellery, crossed Wilhelmstrasse, and went through the Brandenburg Gate, opened to the West, and crowned by a partially broken statue of the goddess of victory, a symbol of the old world. Let us now quote a longer excerpt of Pierre Rostaing's memoirs, as he so vividly depicts the tragedy of those first moments after capture: "We move forward, our hands up in the air, towards a group of Red Army soldiers who surrounded us.

Germania's Assault Generation

They were Mongols. Without any questions, they took away our watches and put them on. I saw that some of them had ten of those on each hand. Then they regrouped us on a square nearby, hitting our backs with sticks. I'm so tired, their brutality doesn't even phase me.

There they searched us more thoroughly. They took everything we had in our pockets: papers, pictures, money, jewelry. Constantly, we could hear only one question: "You SS? Destroy tanks? You SS? Destroy tanks?" We didn't respond. Luckily, we got rid of our insignia earlier, leaving only the epaulettes. One of us, however, forgot to remove the two tiny silver tanks, symbolizing the T-34s he had destroyed. A Mongolian officer saw it, and flew into a rage. He yelled, waved his arms around, striking with his fists and feet. Then, without observing any kind of protocol, just took out his gun and shot our friend in the head. The man was the last to fall in the battle for Berlin. There were only sixteen of us left! Was that impromptu execution not a war crime? I ask this of those who believed themselves to be judges in 1945. Back then, though, I did not ask that question. I thought that'd be all our fate. The Russians had an odd way of treating prisoners of war! Standing in a row by a wall, the Mongols aiming their machine guns at our heads, we were sure it was our last hour. Me, who had spent 15 years in the colonies, three years in the German Army, escaping all the traps unharmed, I was furious I would have to die defenseless. I was oddly calm, though. I've already said goodbye to my life. On my right, an 18 year old guy, Kapar, was crying. He had shown extraordinary courage in battle, but this time he lost control. I was able to muster up enough strength to comfort him: "Don't cry, now, you'll see. You won't even notice. It's gonna be quick." Fenet was no longer with us. Because he was an officer, they took him away right after we surrendered. There's 15 of us, and with our hearts in our throats, we wait for death. Suddenly a completely drunken Russian officer appeared. He was holding a

Götterdämmerung - the Last Moments of the 33.Waffen-Grenadier-Division der SS - "Charlemagne"

bottle in his arms, walking in a zigzag. Finally, he stopped mere 5 m from me and asked in Russian: "What's this?" Luckily, I knew the language so I was able to respond, "We're Frenchmen." This started an odd dialogue. "So what are you doing dressed up like this?" - "Germans got us and forced us into the army." - "That true?" – "Nothing could be more true." I must have been convincing because he ordered the Mongolians to put their guns down and sent them away. He said to me, "Tell your men to line up and follow me." We approached a prisoner convoy nearby. It was headed up by a truck, carrying speakers, playing marching songs. We hung our heads and followed the car. Such a weird guide we had! In this company we arrived at the huge Tempelhof airport. There were already numerous German POWs there, prisoners of all nations, workers, and civilians. So many people under the Red Army's rule. We remained there for almost an hour, while they counted us. I supposed Russians liked doing that. After that, we were on our way again, escorted by soldiers with rough faces. We passed Berlin. Civilians stood on the sidewalks, trying to spot their brothers, husbands, or friends. Tears trickled down their cheeks, as they repeated their mantra: "Poor boys. Poor boys." When night came, we set up camp in the eastern part of the capital, on a factory square, near a small river. It was cold. We didn't have food or blankets. The Russians seemed disinterested in our fate. We couldn't sleep. The thickening fog went deep into our bones. Sitting on a pile of rocks, patting my back to warm myself up, I shivered until dawn, unable to form a coherent thought. We moved out again. The wounded and stragglers were mercilessly killed by the guards; bullets put into their heads. The way was strewn with the wreckage of T-34 tanks; chopped up pine trees still showed bullet holes; signs along the roads told the story of Russian victories. Early in the afternoon, a Rollbahn official came, unnoticed at first until the Russians mistook him for an SS general, because of the helmet with green rim, and they mowed him down with machine guns. Before that, however, the man got lynched by a mob of brutal communist thugs. Even at the worst moments of our Russian campaign, I never saw such cruel hate among our LVF as the one shown by the Red Army. You could say that, later on, some would ignorantly say that it was civilization's victory over barbarity! Years later, Krukenberg thus summed up the French Volunteers of the Waffen SS and their actions in the Battle for Berlin: "Without the Frenchmen, the Russians would've taken Berlin eight days earlier!" Certainly. They are credited with the destruction of 50-60 enemy tanks!

Berlin, 1945 – "Fight until the end..."

Endnote - The Waffen SS

Himmler, wishing to expand the Waffen SS, advocated the idea of SS-controlled foreign legions. The Reichsführer, with his penchant for medieval lore, envisioned a united European "crusade", fighting to save old Europe from the "Godless Bolshevik hordes." While volunteers from regions which had been declared Aryan were approved almost instantly, Himmler eagerly pressed for the creation of more and more foreign units.

In late 1940, the creation of a multinational SS Division, the Wiking, was authorized. Command of the division was given to SS-Brigadeführer Felix Steiner. Steiner immersed himself in the organization of the volunteer division, soon becoming a strong advocate for an increased number of foreign units. The Wiking was committed to combat several days after the launch of Operation Barbarossa, proving itself an impressive fighting unit. Soon Danish, French, Azeri, Armenian, Flemish, Norwegian, Finnish, and Dutch "Freiwilligen" (volunteer) formations were committed to combat, gradually proving their worth. Among the more unusual units to exist in the Waffen SS was the American Free Corps or "George Washington Brigade." Its most famous member was Second Lieutenant Martin James Monti, who worked as a propaganda broadcaster, as well. The "American Free Corps" consisted of no more than five members. Another unit, the Britisches Freikorps, a unit composed of citizens of the British Commonwealth, was led by John Amery, and had a strength of no more than 60 men. Still another unit, the Indian National Army, was composed of Indian troops, mostly prisoners of war recruited by the Germans. Hitler however, was hesitant to allow foreign volunteers to be formed into formations based on their ethnicity, preferring that they be absorbed into multi-national divisions. Hitler feared that unless the foreign recruits were committed to the idea of a united Germania, then their reasons for fighting were suspect, and could damage the German cause.

Himmler was allowed to create his new formations, but they were to be commanded by German officers and NCOs. Beginning in 1942 - 1943, several new formations were formed from Bosnians, Latvians, Estonians, and Ukrainians. The Reichsführer had sidestepped the race laws by ordering that Waffen SS units formed with men from non-Aryan backgrounds were to be designated as, "Division der SS" (or Division of the SS) rather than SS Division. The wearing of the SS runes on the collar was forbidden, with several of these formations wearing national insignia instead.

All non-Germanic officers and men in these units had their rank prefix changed from "SS" to "Waffen" (e.g., a Latvian Hauptscharführer would be referred to as a Waffen-Hauptscharführer, rather than SS-Hauptscharführer). An example of a Division der SS is the Estonian 20.Waffen-Grenadier-Division der SS (estnische Nr.1). The combat ability of the Divisions der SS varied greatly, with the Latvian, French, Flemish, and Estonian formations performing exceptionally, whilst the Albanian units performed poorly.

While many adventurers and idealists joined the SS as part of the fight against Communism, many of the later recruits joined or were conscripted for different reasons. For example, Dutchmen who joined the 34.SS-Freiwilligen-Grenadier-Division Landstorm Nederland were granted exemption from forced labor and provided with food, pay, and accommodation. Recruits who joined for such reasons rarely proved good soldiers, and several units composed of such volunteers were involved in atrocities.

Endnote - The Waffen SS

Towards the end of 1943, it became apparent that numbers of volunteer recruits were inadequate to meet the needs of the German military, so conscription was introduced. The Estonian 20.Waffen-Grenadier-Division der SS (estnische Nr.1) is an example of such a conscript formation, which proved to be outstanding soldiers with an unblemished record.

Not satisfied with the growing number of volunteer formations, Himmler sought to gain control of all volunteer forces serving alongside Germany. This put the SS at odds with the Heer, as several volunteer units had been placed under Heer control (e.g., volunteers of the Spanish Blue Division or the 373rd [*Wallonische*] Infantry Battalion which was transferred under SS command in June 1943). Despite this, Himmler constantly campaigned to have all foreign volunteers fall under the SS banner. In several cases, like the ROA (*Russkaya osvoboditel'naya armiya* or Russian Liberation Army) and the 5.SS-Freiwilligen-Sturmbrigade Wallonien, he was successful. By the last year of the war, most foreign volunteers units did fall under SS command. While several volunteer units performed poorly in combat, the majority acquitted themselves well. French and Spanish SS volunteers, along with remnants of the 11.SS-Freiwilligen-Panzergrenadier-Division Nordland, formed the final defense of the Reichshauptstadt in 1945.

After the surrender, many volunteers were tried and imprisoned by their countries. In several cases, volunteers were executed. Those volunteers from the Baltic States and Ukraine could at best look forward to years spent in the Gulags. To avoid this, many ex-volunteers from these regions joined underground resistance groups, which were engaged fighting the Soviets until the 1950s.

In Estonia and Latvia, the majority of the Waffen SS veterans were conscripts who were at least partly considered freedom fighters.

Germania's Assault Generation

An April 13, 1950 message from the U.S. High Commission in Germany (HICOG), signed by General Frank McCloy to the Secretary of State, clarified the US position on the "Baltic Legions": they were not to be seen as "movements", "volunteer", or "SS". In short, they were not given the training, indoctrination, and induction normally given to SS members. The U.S. Displaced Persons Commission in September 1950 subsequently declared that the Baltic Waffen SS Units (Baltic Legions) are to be considered as separate and distinct in purpose, ideology, activities, and qualifications for membership from the German SS, and therefore the Commission holds them not to be a movement hostile to the Government of the United States. Still, much debate continues on this issue, and because of general condemnation of the Nazi regime across the globe, official statements of the position of Estonian and Latvian Waffen SS veterans remains ambiguous. The Latvian parliament Saeima declared "the day of the Legion" (16 March) as a national holiday, but under pressure from the European Union, reversed its decision in 2000. Overall, around 60% of Waffen SS members were non-German.

The SS never, even under the most desperate situations, turned their collective back on their members. In this they were considerably more admirable than say the Japanese armed forces, in general (who regarded themselves as being the Knights of Bushido). There are instances of Japanese soldiers being denied aid because they were from a different unit from which those they sought assistance. A good example of this was during the Battle for Okinawa. Towards the end, as the cohesiveness of the defense collapsed, desperate soldiers from destroyed units were turned away to go and fend for themselves by other more fortunate groups.

Following the German surrender in May 1945, the whole of the SS was declared an illegal organization. This blanket condemnation was issued without any distinction between its various parts. Thus the

Endnote - The Waffen SS

Gestapo was judged as guilty as the SS-Signals Corps (and vice-versa). This arbitrary and universal condemnation gave rise to a somewhat unexpected and unintentional result: the German people as a whole took the opportunity to lay all the blame for the excesses of The Third Reich onto the SS, and avoid any personal responsibility of their own. There is an early book about this phenomenon by Gerald Reitlinger, called, *"The SS Alibi of a Nation."*

In effect, the Allies created a convenient whipping boy out of the SS (both the Waffen SS and Allgemeine SS), which allowed ordinary Germans to conveniently forget that they had earlier voted and cheered enthusiastically for Hitler and the Nazi Party. It must be re-stated that the Nazis had been voted democratically into power on the promises laid down in a clearly stated set of proposals. On this basis, all Germans of voting age in 1933 have to accept that they share some measure of responsibility for what followed; to pass all the blame to the SS was (and still is) simply wrong.

To demonize individual members of the SS simply because they were members of the SS is a gross injustice, yet an entire country (France) did just that after the war when they passed "The Law of Collective Responsibility". This act said that all members of a unit that had carried out a war crime were to be regarded as equally suspect, and indeed equally guilty, unless they could prove their non-involvement. Thus all members of the 3rd Company of the 1st Battalion of the Der Führer Regiment of Das Reich were to be regarded as being equally culpable for the events at Oradour.

Recruiting

In July 1940, the SS began an active program to gain Western European recruits from newly-conquered countries for several new Waffen SS volunteer legions. This effort intensified after June 1941, as the SS exhorted volunteers to join the "anti-Bolshevik" campaign in the Soviet Union. Enlistment rolls show that more than 125,000 West Europeans volunteered of their own free will to join the Waffen SS. Eastern Europeans, numbering another 220,000 - primarily from the Baltic States and the Ukraine - also joined the Waffen SS. Despite the SS belief in the superiority of the German race, the decline in German military fortunes caused the SS to quietly shelve their racist beliefs about "Untermenschen" in favor of the more practical policy of recruiting these essentially Slavic peoples to fight against the Soviets. These foreign units were often armed from stores of captured or substandard equipment. Their training tended to be more haphazard. Basic training lasted as short as two or three weeks. Unlike most armies, no "parade ground training" was conducted, being replaced with aggressive live fire exercises with real ammunition. The recruits were also exposed to multiple combined arms training, such as artillerymen would learn how to use radios, signals troops would learn how to fire heavy machine guns, etc.

These foreign fighters were treated differently from the German troops in the SS. They took a slightly different oath of service upon enlisting, and often wore unique insignia or ethnic uniforms. Language differences were always a barrier, with most units being led by regular German SS officers who often treated their men as something like second class citizens. Former Waffen SS volunteer Albert Olbrechts stated that when his group of the Flemish Legion just arrived in their training camp in Debica in Poland, the first thing the German SS officer said: "Look at this bunch of gypsies! Do you really think we're going to use you? Probably you only came here to eat and to shit!" They were exposed to less Nazi indoctrination, and the Nazi propaganda was tailored to their nationality. They were often partly motivated by their own political or nationalistic agendas.

Himmler ordered that new Waffen SS units formed with men of non-Germanic ethnicity were to be designated Division der SS (or

Endnote - The Waffen SS

Division of the SS), rather than SS Division. The wearing of the SS runes on the collar was typically not done, with several of these formations wearing a unique national insignia instead. For example, in the spring of 1941 a second Germanic Regiment was raised, the SS Infantry Regiment "Nordwest", composed of Dutch, Flemish, and Danish volunteers. Unlike the volunteers in the Westland Regiment who wore SS collar tabs, the volunteers in the Nordwest were granted the distinction of their own special collar tab of a three-legged swastika, referred to as a trident sun wheel or trifos.

By September 1941, the Nordwest was disbanded, and its personnel distributed to their respective ethnic legion formation. Many of the transferees from the disbanded Nordwest continued to wear their trifos collar tab for a time in their respective ethnic legions. Some units even wore non-standard uniforms. For example, the 13.Waffen-Gebirgsjäger-Division der SS (kroatische Nr.1) "Handschar" had its Bosnian Muslim soldiers wear a Fez hat with the Totenkopf insignia attached to it. Soldiers of non-German citizenship in these units had their rank prefix changed from SS to Waffen (e.g., a Serbian Hauptscharführer would be referred to as a Waffen-Hauptscharführer rather than SS-Hauptscharführer). The combat ability of the SS Divisions varied greatly. For example, the Norwegian, French and Estonian formations performed exceptionally, while the Albanian and Ukrainian units performed poorly. Some of these units were formed for propaganda purposes only, such as the British Free Corps, which was raised from British prisoners of war, and was generally kept from combat operations.

Some of these foreign volunteer units/divisions were often the most disciplined and fanatic of SS troopers. Their combat reputations ranged from excellent to fair. Units such as Nordland, Leon Degrelle's Walloon Legion, and Langemarck contained Europeans that volunteered for service in the "anti-Bolshevik" crusade against

213

the Soviet Union. Waffen SS troops as a whole earned a distinguished combat reputation during WWII, renowned for both stunning offensive victories and tenacious defensive operations. Without question, many SS troops exhibited incredible feats of bravery, courage, and tactical brilliance, throughout the duration of the conflict. While many infantry units fought on the front lines, more were often relegated to security duty and anti-partisan sweeps. This type of service against guerilla bands who themselves took no prisoners, lead to many atrocities. The combat record of several of these units such as the 29.Waffen-Grenadier-Division der SS (rußische Nr.1 also known as "R.O.N.A.") on such Sühnemassnahmen or "atonement operations" was often too grisly even for military journalists to cover, and stains the Waffen SS to this day in a portrait of horror.

Late in the war as Germany's hope of victory waned, these volunteers fought harder and more recklessly. Considered traitors by their countrymen, they had no home to return to. These men with nothing left to lose became the worst sort of man you wanted to encounter on the battlefield. These units typically fought into extinction, refusing to surrender for fears they would be repatriated to their home countries. Thousands of Russian Cossacks serving in the SS Kosaken-Kavallerie-Korps were executed when turned over to Soviet troops, as were members of the Serbian Volunteer Corps when turned over to Tito's Partisans. More moderate countries such as Norway, Denmark, and Britain jailed their wayward SS volunteers for as many as fifteen years. The purpose of the Waffen SS was to impose Hitler's world view on the greater European continent, and those non-German Europeans that served him often found them living out the rest of their lives in exile: their service to him voiding their pre-war life.

Das Kreuz im Hürtgenwald

Hingelehnt im Tannenholz,
ganz einsam und verlassen,
steht ein schlichtes Birkenkreuz
Wind und Wetter überlassen.

Schon viele Jahre steht es dort
mit einem Stahlhelm nur bedacht,
erinnert uns an jenen Ort,
wo einst ein Krieger hat gewacht.

Mit seinem Blut hat er getränkt
im tiefen Wald die kühle Erde.
Wir bitten Gott, der alles lenkt,
dass niemand ihn vergessen werde.

Geopfert für das Vaterland
hat er sein höchstes Gut - das Leben.
Kein Mensch kann außer Gotteshand
ihm dieses jemals wiedergeben.

So schlafe wohl, fern von den Lieben,
bis wir uns einmal wieder sehen,
wo dich gebettet, die geblieben,
da wirst du wieder aufersteh'n.

In Memoriam:

Rösch, Helmut - SS-Uscha - St.Kp.Pz.A.A. L.SS.A.H. - KIA on December 1, 1944

Samisch, Manfred - SS-Mann - unit/division unknown - KIA November 23, 1944

Schneider, Josef - SS-Oscha - unit/division unknown - KIA on December 23, 1944

Schweiger, Leonhard - SS-Mann - I/SS.Pz.Korps I.St.A.H. Fla.Kp. - KIA on December 12, 1944

Stück, Karl - SS-Grenadier - unit/division unknown - KIA on December 14, 1944

Bognich, Harry - SS-Panzergrenadier - 1.SS.Pz.Gr.R.G. L.SS.A.H.; SS.Pz.Gren.A.u.E.Batl. - KIA on December 12, 1944

Fenners, Christian - SS-Panzergrenadier - 1.SS.Pz.Gr.R. L.SS.A.H. - KIA on December 11, 1944

Schwabe, Erich - SS-Mann - 1/SS PZ G.E.BTL Totenkopf I; SS Panzerdivision Hohenstaufen - KIA on January 7, 1945

The 38 Divisions of the Waffen SS

The following is a list of all the Waffen SS Divisions from the period 1939-1945. It must be recognized that some divisions actually never reached the strength of a Division.

1.SS-Panzer-Division - "Leibstandarte-SS Adolf Hitler"

2.SS-Panzer-Division - "Das Reich"

3.SS-Panzer-Division - "Totenkopf"

4.SS-Polizei-Panzergrenadier-Division - "SS-Polizei-Division"

5.SS-Panzer-Division - "Wiking"

6.SS-Gebirgsjäger-Division - "Nord"

7.SS-Freiwilligen-Gebirgsjäger-Division - "Prinz Eugen"

8.SS-Kavallerie-Division - "Florian Geyer"

9.SS-Panzer-Division - "Hohenstaufen"

10.SS-Panzer-Division - "Frundsberg"

11.SS-Freiwilligen-Panzergrenadier-Division - "Nordland"

12.SS-Panzer-Division - "Hitlerjugend"

Germania's Assault Generation

13.Waffen-Gebirgsjäger-Division der SS (kroatische Nr.1) - "Handschar"

14.Waffen-Grenadier-Division der SS (galizische / ukrainische Nr.1) - "Galizien"

15.Waffen-Grenadier-Division der SS (lettische Nr.1) - "Lettland"

16.SS-Panzergrenadier-Division - "Reichsführer-SS"

17.SS-Panzergrenadier-Division - "Götz von Berlichingen"

18.SS-Freiwilligen-Panzergrenadier-Division "Horst Wessel"

19.Waffen-Grenadier-Division der SS (lettische Nr.2) - "Latvia"

20.Waffen-Grenadier-Division der SS (estnische Nr.1) - "Estland"

21.Waffen-Gebirgsjäger-Division der SS (albanische Nr.1) - "Skanderbeg"

22.SS-Freiwilligen-Kavallerie-Division - "Maria Theresa" (ungarische)

23.SS-Freiwilligen-Panzergrenadier-Division (niederländische Nr.1) - "Nederland"

23.Waffen-Gebirgsjäger-Division der SS (kroatische Nr.2) - "Kama"

24.Waffen-Gebirgsjäger-Division der SS - "Karstjäger"

The 38 Divisions of the Waffen SS

25.Waffen-Grenadier-Division der SS (ungarische Nr.1) - "Hunyadi"

26.Waffen-Grenadier-Division der SS (ungarische Nr.2) - "Hungaria"

27.SS-Freiwilligen-Grenadier-Division (flämische Nr.1) - "Langemarck"

28.SS-Freiwilligen-Grenadier-Division - "Wallonien"

29.Waffen-Grenadier-Division der SS (italienische Nr.1) - "Italien"

29.Waffen-Grenadier-Division der SS (rußische Nr.1) (also "R.O.N.A.")

30.Waffen-Grenadier-Division der SS (rußische Nr.2)

30.Waffen-Grenadier-Division der SS (weißruthenische Nr.1) - "Weißruthenien"

31.SS-Freiwilligen-Grenadier-Division - "Batschka"

32.SS-Freiwilligen-Grenadier-Division - "30 Januar"

33.Waffen-Grenadier-Division der SS (französische Nr.1) - "Charlemagne"

33.Waffen-Kavallerie-Division der SS (ungarische Nr.3)

Germania's Assault Generation

34.SS-Freiwilligen-Grenadier-Division - "Landstorm Nederland"
(niederländische Nr.2)

35.SS-Polizei-Grenadier-Division - "SS-Polizei-Division II"

36.Waffen-Grenadier-Division der SS - "Dirlewanger"

37.SS-Freiwilligen-Kavallerie-Division - "Lützow"

38.SS-Grenadier-Division - "Nibelungen"

****

References - Sources

Introduction

Steiner, Die Freiwilligen der Waffen-SS, 42, 68, 80. Felix Steiner, Die Freiwilligen der Waffen-SS: Idee und Opfergang (Preuss. Oldendorf: Verlag K. W. Schültz KG 1958).

Claus Bundgård Christensen, Niels Bo Poulsen and Peter Scharff Smith, Under hagekors og Dannebrog: Danskere i Waffen SS 1940–45, 2nd edition (Copenhagen: Aschehoug 2002), 87.

Terje Emberland and Matthew Kott, Himmlers Norge: Nordmenn I det storgermanske prosjekt (Oslo: Aschehoug 2012), 237–47 (246); George Stein, Geschichte der Waffen-SS (Düsseldorf: DrosteVerlag 1967), 245; Ola Flyum, 'Olav Tuff (91): Vi brente en kirke med sivilister', 1 October 2013

Karsten Wilke, Die 'Hilfsgemeinschaft auf Gegenseitigkeit' (HIAG): Veteranen der Waffen-SS in der Bundesrepublik (Paderborn: Schöningh 2011).

'Hinweis zur erbrechtlichenVerfügung', in the organization's newsletter Kriegsgräberstiftung—Wenn alle Brüder schweigen, Mitteilungsblatt, no. 2, May 2004.

Peter Strassner, Europäische Freiwillige: Geschichte die 5. SS-Panzer-division Wiking (Osnabrück: Munin Verlag 1968), 84; Christensen, Poulsen and Smith, Under hagekors og Dannebrog, 110–12.

The International Military Tribunal, 1946: Vol. 20:367

Stabswache de Euros – Robert Lee – Quote about the Waffen SS last paragraph of the intro

The Legionnaires

Steffen Werther, SS-Vision und Grenzland-Realität: Vom Umgang dänischer und 'volksdeutscher' Nationalsozialisten in Sønderjylland mit der 'großgermanischen' Ideologie der SS (Stockholm: Acta Universitatis Stockholmiensis 2012), 134–5.

Heinrich Himmler, Geheimreden 1933–45 und andere Ansprachen, ed. Bradley Smith and Agnes Peterson (Frankfurt am Main: Propyläen Verlag 1974), 38–49; Josef Ackermann, Heinrich Himmler als Ideologe (Göttingen: Musterschmidt 1970), 276–84; N.K.C.A. in't Veld (ed.), De SS en Nederland: Documenten uit SS-Archieven 1935–1945, vol. 1 (The Hague: Nijhoff 1976), Doc. 209, 804.

Germania's Assault Generation

'Richtlinien für das III. Germanische Panzerkorps', 25 May 1943, Doc. 9, in Bernd Wegner, 'Auf dem Wege zur pangermanischen Armee: Dokumente zum III (Germanische) SS-Panzerkorps', Militärgeschichtliche Mitteilungen, vol. 28, 1980, 101–36 (123–4).

Himmler's speech, 29 February 1940, quoted in Himmler, Geheimreden 1933–45 und andere Ansprachen, 142.

Gottlob Berger quote from Bernd Wegner, Hitlers Politische Soldaten: Die Waffen-SS 1933–1945 (Paderborn: Schöningh 2006), 298.

Leon Degrelle after action report d.d. February 18 – 1945; copy of the original document provided and used with permission of Tomasz Borowski. Text in French translated by the author.

Martti Lehtonen

Story provided by Jaana Lehtonen (his granddaughter) as well as the permission to use it. Text/diary initially translated from the Finnish language into English by Ville Hacklin; reviewed and modified for this book by the author.

Mr. Mauno Jokipii, Finnish professor of history, has written a complete history of the Finnish volunteers and their battalion. He had written also other studies about European volunteers and about the history of Finland in general. These works of Prof. Mauno Jokipii were the most valuable sources when information about Finnish volunteers was needed and those were also used in this writing.

Martti Lehtonen's diary and letters

Interviews with the Finnish volunteer SS-battalion veterans and their written memoirs

Literature sources:

Register of the Waffen-SS Finnish Volunteer Battalion, The Veljesapu-Perinneyhdistys heritage association, ISBN 978-952-93-1930, 2013

Hitlerin Saksa ja sen vapaaehtoisliikkeet, Mauno Jokipii, SKS, ISBN 978-951-746-335-5

Panttipataljoona – Suomalaisen SS-pataljoonan historia, Mauno Jokipii, Gummers Oy, ISBN 952-90-7363-1, Fourth edition, 2000

References

A war volunteer in the Hitlerjugend Division

"Willi Witte: Hitler-Jugend und Kriegserlebnisse in Sylt" – used with the kind permission of Oliver Schweinoch of the LEMO – Lebendiges Museum Online - Deutsches Historisches Museum - translated by the author.

From the Frw. Standarte Nordwest to the Germanic SS in Flanders

Van Dijck story obtained through personal correspondence with Tony. Extra information obtained through the SMF and Van Dijck before the SMF was disbanded.

Schwerer Granatwerfer Zug – 4.Kp/I. Btl/67. Rgt/III. SS-Panzer-Korps

Story from Dries Coolens – personal correspondence including many phone interviews with the author

A War Volunteer with the Hitlerjugend Division

Witte, Willi: Kriegserlebenisse in der Waffen SS; SS Kriegsgefangenenlager Plattlingen; Flucht und Gefangenschaft, in: LeMO-Zeitzeugen, Lebendiges Museum Online, Stiftung Haus der Geschichte der Bundesrepublik Deutschland

From Demjansk to Breslau

Story provided by Herr Schoenfeld via personal correspondence with the author. Herr Schoenfeld was also so kind to provide me with a signed picture of him.

Hunting Soviet Panzers on the Eastern Front

#153 Wir jagen Sowjetpanzer - Kriegsbücherei der deutschen Jugend. Document is part of the author's collection and was fully translated by the author from German into English.

Germania's Assault Generation

Götterdämmerung - the Last Moments of the 33.Waffen-Grenadier-Division der SS - "Charlemagne"

Text provided by Tomasz Borowski and used with his permission. Text was slightly modified by the author

The Ministry of Aviation was a command post for Seifert. The Frenchmen were defending the Ministry of Security (RSHA) on Prinz-Albrechtstrasse.

According to Le Tissier, Ziegler was in Wilhelm Mohnke's group and was fatally wounded on Ivalidenstrasse. Mabire, however, believes he was killed in the same group but on Albrechtstrasse

Forbes Robert, op.cit.

Saint-Loup, op.cit., p. 494.

Saint-Loup, op.cit., p. 495.

Berger Henri, op.cit., p. 34.

Fenet Henri, op.cit.

Saint-Loup, op.cit., p.493.

Lefèvre Eric, op.cit.

Saint-Loup, op.cit., p. 508.

Rostaing Pierre, op.cit., p. 203.

Fenet Henri, op.cit., p. 30.

According to Saint-Loup, Brunet attracted attention because he had four silver badges on his uniform jacket for the tanks he'd destroyed. Because so many Russian's tank-men died during the Battle for Berlin, their surviving comrades could take offence to that.

Brunet was certainly the last Frenchman to die in Battle for Berlin.

Lefèvre Eric, op.cit., p.29

Rostaing Pierre, op.cit. p. 211-212

Endnote

Dich Ruft die SS – H. Hillger Verlag 1942 - Verantwortlicher Herausgeber: Der ReichsführerSS - SS-Hauptamt, berlin-Wilmersdorf 1, Hohenzollerndamm 31 – copy of Dich Ruft die SS is from the personal collection of the author.

Research on the Waffen SS topic through the following websites, books and libraries:

The private library of the Sint Maartensfonds (SMF) in Antwerp, Belgium – HQ in the Van Maerlantstraat. Toon Pauli, Alfons Janssens, Tony Van Dijck, Dries Coolens, and Dries Decru – all former Waffen SS members and personal friends – who were so kind to tell me their personal stories and to give me access to this library.

The monthly magazine "Berkenkruis" of the Sint Maartensfonds.

The European Volunteer Movement in World War II by Richard Landwehr

References

All pictures in this book are obtained through open source media, except the pictures of Martti Lehtonen. The pictures found on open source media are not the property of a specific body or entity. Tracking the original owner of these pictures is as good as impossible. Pictures are used as a reference for this book and are not specific to the soldier's story. Certain pictures were obtained by the Bundesarchiv in Germany and are marked "Bundesarchiv…" Pictures of Martti Lehtonen are property of Jaana Lehtonen, who owns the copyright on them as well. Reproduction of the pictures of Martti Lehtonen is strictly prohibited.

Picture on the first page: SS symbol; picture on the last page: black sun.

Cover created by Andrea Sysyphus.

All interviews/stories or parts of it were used with kind permission of the interviewer/interviewee/author. All original stories that were provided in the German, Dutch, or French language have been translated by the author. Translation from Finnish to English by Ville Hacklin.

All stories written in this book are from WWII Waffen SS veterans. Most of the names of these veterans have been replaced by a fictional name to protect the veterans and their families. Some of the stories were given to me with the request never to disclose the personal information of the veteran. Let it be clear that the real names of all these veterans will never be disclosed and that all email requests asking for disclosure will be ignored and deleted immediately. This is my loyalty as a writer towards these men and their families who trusted me with their personal stories of that era. This book is intended to be an historical account of WWII and it doesn't support the ideologies of the Third Reich and its affiliates.

****

Germania's Assault Generation

ISBN-13: 978-1512331486
ISBN-10: 1512331481
BISAC: History / Military / World War II

You can contact the author at
ghost-division@outlook.com

Published in the United States of America - 2017

References

24223804R00134

Printed in Great Britain
by Amazon